A FIELD GUIDE TO
*Dangerous Animals*
*of North America*

A FIELD GUIDE TO

# Dangerous Animals of North America

INCLUDING CENTRAL AMERICA

## CHARLES K. LEVY, Ph.D.
Professor of Biology, Boston University

Illustrations by L. Laszlo Meszoly

Text photographs by Frederica Matera

THE STEPHEN GREENE PRESS
Brattleboro, Vermont
Lexington, Massachusetts

We are grateful to the following photographers for their permission to include their color photographs in the color illustration section: Plates 1–8, 12, 13, 15, 16, 18, 19, 22, 24, 28, 31 © Frederick Dodd; Plates 9, 10, 17 © Joseph T. Collins; Plate 11 © Charles Levy; Plate 14 © Frederica Matera; Plates 20, 21, 26 © Fred Bavendam; Plate 23 H. Wes Pratt, U.S. Government, N.O.A.A. photo; Plate 27 © Les Kauffman; Plates 29, 30 © Jeff Rotman; Plates 32, 33 © Dr. James Traniello.

FIRST EDITION

Text and line illustrations copyright © 1983 by The Stephen Greene Press

Black and white text photographs copyright © 1983 by Frederica Matera

This book is manufactured in the United States of America. It is designed by Irving Perkins Associates and published by The Stephen Greene Press, Fessenden Road, Brattleboro, Vermont 05301.

**Library of Congress Cataloging in Publication Data**

Levy, Charles K., 1924-
    A field guide to dangerous animals of North America including Central America.

    Bibliography: p. 160
    Includes index.
    1. Dangerous animals—North America.  2. Dangerous animals—Central America.  3. First aid in illness and injury.  I. Title.
QL100.L48 1983        796.5′028′9        83–1440
ISBN 0–8289–0503–7 (pbk.)

# Contents

## List of Color Plates

These color plates follow page 84.

# Introduction

Due to increased mobility, the number of people who hike, camp, fish, snorkle, scuba dive, or hunt in the great outdoors is increasing by leaps and bounds. This field guide provides readers with a concise survey of annoying or dangerous animals and advises how to avoid them. Further, it provides the most recent and accurate methods of first aid and medical treatment, should it be needed. Knowing the regions these creatures inhabit and when they are apt to be encountered is important and this information is included. Within the six sections each of the animals is described in some detail; unlike the usual field guide only major anatomical features are stressed. Black and white drawings of each animal accompany the text, and thirty-three color photographs highlight some of the more interesting ones. Indeed, some of the deadliest animals are highly visible—their bright colors a sign of danger. Once the eye is trained, one is better able to avoid these species.

Since antiquity people have been fascinated with animals that bite, sting, poison, or otherwise envenomate humans. It is important at this point to define the difference between poisoning and envenomation. Animals that envenomate have glands that produce and store one or several poisons and have a poison delivery apparatus, a fang or spine with which this poison is injected. In this sense, all animals that envenomate are poisonous. Here, the term poisonous animals refers to those animals that produce or concentrate poisons in some of their tissues and cause reactions only when eaten or touched. Finally some animals are dangerous because they can bite, maul, or scratch. Attacks on humans by biting animals are quite rare; the popular media tends to blow their incidence out of proportion. Dogs are responsible for most bites (over six hundred thousand); their attacks result in six to ten deaths per year. Bears, sharks, barracudas, crocodiles, and other biters cause fewer than two hundred attacks per year and less than ten deaths in North America.

Thousands of species are either always or occasionally poisonous or venomous. Generally such poisonings are the result of accidental encounters, but there are some species that do selectively attack humans: mosquitoes, bedbugs, and other blood-sucking organisms. Most attacks, literally tens of millions per year, are attributed to venomous arthropods (insects, spiders, and scorpions) and the majority of these occur in warm tropic or subtropical areas or in temperate climates during the summer. The impact is not trivial since in North and Central America there may be over a thousands deaths (most attributed to Mexican scorpions) and twenty-five to forty thousand envenomations that produce symptoms severe enough to warrant medical treatment. However, most arthropods described in this book simply cause us annoyance, a tolerable amount of pain, itchiness, and sleepless nights. There are also a number of water-dwelling animals usually found in salt water that can envenomate, bite, or are poisonous to eat. While deaths are really quite rare, a number of these marine organisms can make us very ill or very uncomfortable. Then there are the poisonous reptiles that frighten so many of us. Actually, reptile envenomations are rare, probably less than seven thousand per year, and they are seldom fatal, only fifteen to twenty-five per year in the United States, and twenty-five to fifty per year in Central America. However, most venomous snake bites should be treated as medical emergencies, and if untreated can cause serious tissue loss or death.

Proper first aid and medical treatment of envenomation and poisoning is obscured by myth and blatant misinformation. Even symptoms of envenomation are confused by folklore. Here we provide the most accurate description of symptoms; these symptoms are most essential for determining medical treatment. To provide this information, no fewer than four hundred references were consulted, most original clinical or research reports, and it was evident that there is considerable controversy over both first aid and treatment. Fortunately there are two outstanding specialists in animal poisoning who provided the guidelines and recommendations incorporated in this field guide. The first is Dr. Bruce W. Halstead, M.D., who, for the past four decades, has studied and written on dangerous marine organisms. His writings are highly recommended for anyone wishing to know more about dangerous marine animals. The second major source for information regarding symptoms, first aid, and medical treatment is Dr. Findlay E. Russell, M.D., Ph.D. Dr. Russell is certainly the most qualified expert on the treatment of envenomations. He is a scholar-researcher with a vast knowledge of animal toxins and a clinician as well. He and his colleagues have vast experience in dealing with the treatment of snake bites and envenomation by other stinging animals. Dr. Russell has written a number of books and papers on the subject and readers wishing to obtain more detailed information should turn to his works.

# Acknowledgments

An effort has been made here to interest the reader and to simplify the scientific and medical jargon. Dr. Charles Weingarten, Chief of Medicine at McLean Hospital, was kind enough to help me make sense of the medical definitions. My former colleague Dr. Peter Oldak, M.D., a herpetologist and specialist in emergency medicine, was also of great assistance. His review and suggestions were most welcome. Professor Jamie Traniello, Ph.D., an entomologist at Boston University, provided helpful reviews and suggestions. The outstanding artwork was provided by L. Laszlo Meszoly, a biological illustrator for the Harvard Museum of Comparative Zoology. The anatomically accurate art highlights key features in a way that cannot be achieved with photographs. The beautiful black and white photographs found in the text were provided by Frederica Matera. I also want to thank the fifty-five medical and dental students in the Boston University six-year program for their help in searching the recent medical literature for relevant references.

☠This symbol, as used in this book, indicates that a species has caused known lethalities.

**Note:** Some of the insecticides mentioned in this book are potentially dangerous. Please read manufacturers' directions carefully before using any insecticide.

# PART I
# *Animals Dangerous to Eat*

## BONY FISHES POISONOUS TO EAT
### Ciguatera Poisoning (7–20% ☠ )

Ciguatera fish poisoning is a relatively common illness in tropical marine areas that is caused by the ingestion of any of several fish whose flesh or roe contains a highly toxic substance. The paradox with ciguatera is that a particular kind of fish may be completely edible at one location, but only a few miles down the coast it may be toxic. Over 400 different species of fish may carry ciguatera, and many of these are considered delectable game fish and are commercially important.

The distribution of cigua-toxic fish in tropical marine areas is worldwide. Outbreaks occur most abundantly in the tropical Pacific and the Caribbean in areas roughly between 35 degrees North and 34 degrees South latitude.

The name "ciguatera" derives from the Spanish word for a disease brought on by ingesting a poisonous snail called the cigua. The first reference to ciguatera appears to be by Peter, Martyr of Anghera (1457–1526), the first historian of America. He wrote in 1530 that the fish were made toxic by picking up manchineel apple poison from fruit falling from trees into the local waters.

The source of ciguatera was only discovered in 1979 and is due to a species of microscopic dinoflagellate known as *Gambierdiscus toxicus*. These dinoflagellates live in coral ecosystems in close association with blue-green algae upon which plant-eating bottom-dwelling fish feed. Local coral ecosystems are very sensitive to environmental changes (storms, earthquakes, coastal workings, pollution), and when these occur the dinoflagellate population may rapidly increase. As the dinoflagellate population blooms, the reef fish rapidly accumulate ciguatoxin.

These herbivores are in turn consumed by larger meat-eating fish, and the toxin is concentrated even more. It is from these large carnivores, often desirable game fish, that humans get ciguatera poisoning. Epidemic flare-ups of ciguatera are often

*1*

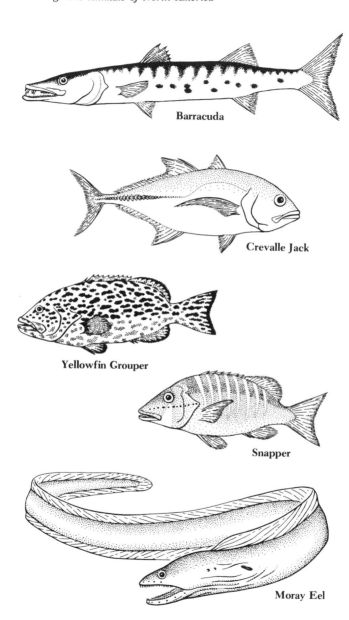

Barracuda

Crevalle Jack

Yellowfin Grouper

Snapper

Moray Eel

associated with localized temporary environmental changes, but fish living on the windward side of oceanic islands are ciguatoxic more or less continuously.

Of the many species of fish that contain ciguatoxin, the blackfin grouper, amberjack, snapper, moray eel, and barracuda are particularly dangerous. (See montage on p. 2.)

Ciguatoxin is a potent nerve poison that is unaffected by cooking or freezing, or storage, and may persist for weeks. It gives no unusual taste, odor, or color to a fish.

Ciguatoxin is now thought to consist of two different parts. The principal toxin, located in skin and muscle, causes stimulation of both the rate and force of contraction of the heart; the main response of the other fraction, selectively concentrated in the digestive system of fish, and practically absent from muscle and skin, is to decrease the heart's contractile activity.

## Symptoms of Ciguatera

There are two groups of symptoms that characterize ciguatera intoxication. Gastrointestinal symptoms, diarrhea (76%), abdominal pain, nausea, and vomiting (68%), occur with maximum intensity about six hours after eating and usually are over in about four to six hours. Then the neurological symptoms begin: numbness, tingling, or burning sensation of the extremities (90%), frequently localized to the palms of the hands and soles of the feet, the lips, and mucosa. There is often a reversal of sensation to hot and cold so that cold objects produce very unpleasant, often acutely painful tingling or burning sensations. These sensory symptoms are the best diagnostic indicator of ciguatera poisoning. Other very frequent symptoms are muscle soreness and joint pain, which occur about 85 percent of the time. Half the people suffering from ciguatoxin also report headache, chills, cramps, itchiness, loss of motor coordination, and dizziness. About a fourth of the victims also reported dental pain, neck stiffness, skin rashes, and watery eyes. The acute illness usually lasts from one to two days; however, the residual weakness and sensory changes can persist for weeks, even years in severe cases. Severity of the illness has a positive relationship to the quantity of fish eaten. However, in a particular group of people who have ingested toxic fish, one may have only a mild gastrointestinal upset, while another may go into respiratory paralysis leading to death. The overall mortality figures usually vary from 7 to 20 percent.

Ciguatera poisoning produces no immunity; rather, more severe illness has been observed in patients experiencing a repeat intoxication. A further problem related to this fact is that after

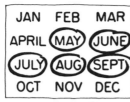

toxin months

 7-20%

duration usually a few days but
neurologic symptoms may
persist for months or years

onset usually 1–6 hrs
75% of cases by 12 hrs
some as much as 30 hrs

**main diagnostic sign 4-8
hrs, numbness, tingling
in mouth, throat, teeth
feel loose, metallic taste**

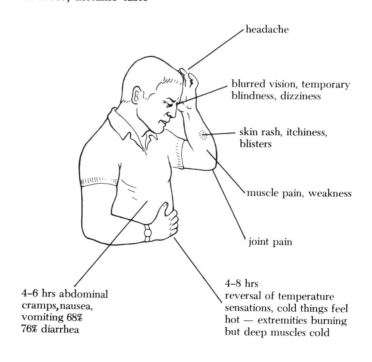

headache

blurred vision, temporary
blindness, dizziness

skin rash, itchiness,
blisters

muscle pain, weakness

joint pain

4–6 hrs abdominal
cramps, nausea,
vomiting 68%
76% diarrhea

4–8 hrs
reversal of temperature
sensations, cold things feel
hot — extremities burning
but deep muscles cold

repeated intoxications, some people seem to develop a hypersensitivity to ciguatera. The result is that they develop ciguatera symptoms after eating fish that has very little or no detectable ciguatoxin. (See illustration on p. 4.)

**Prevention:** Despite many popular folklore stories, there are no effective means of determining if a fish is ciguatoxic.

1. First rule of thumb is to avoid all larger carnivorous fishes. Any big predatory fish weighing more than three pounds is suspect. (See barracuda, p. 33, moray eel, p. 34 and **plates 25 and 26.**)
2. Do not eat digestive organs, gonads, or roe of any potential ciguatoxic fish or large marine turtles. Some toxins concentrate in those organs.
3. Always fish on the leeward side (away from the wind) of large islands, because the windward side is more often the environment that promotes ciguatera.
4. Always check with local fishermen.
5. Poisoning most often occurs in May through September.

**First Aid:** None. If you have ingested a ciguatoxic fish, you will vomit in about six hours anyway.

**Medical Treatment for Ciguatera Poisoning:** Treatment is determined by the specific signs and symptoms that the patient experiences. Resting quietly and cautious sedation are generally advocated to treat the symptoms, along with mechanical respiratory aid when needed. Opiates are suggested for pain and diarrhea. Atropine appears to relieve the cardiovascular signs and symptoms, but has no effect on skeletal muscle symptoms, and only questionable improvement of neurologic manifestations. Following the acute period of one to two days, the best results were obtained from a high protein diet, intravenous vitamin B complex, calcium gluconate, and oral vitamin C, all of which help to lessen the total recuperation time. Diazepam is recommended for insomnia, and analgesic creams and cold showers for pruritus (itching). Furthermore, extremes in temperature which sometimes precipitate painful itching are to be avoided.

## BONY FISHES DANGEROUS TO EAT
### Scombroid Poisoning (Rarely ☠ )

"The Mahimahi Flush" or Scombroid Poisoning is associated with eating spoiled fish of the family Scombroidae. The scombroid fish, mackerels and tunas, are powerful, swift-swimming, streamlined

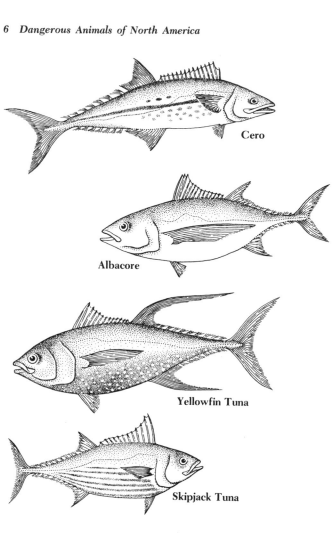

Cero

Albacore

Yellowfin Tuna

Skipjack Tuna

Atlantic Mackerel

(spindle-shaped), muscular fishes with rigid, widely spread tails and distinctive small finlets behind their second dorsal and anal fins. Their bodies are long, and are round in cross section. They have small scales in the region of the head and lower surface.

Included in this family are: the Spanish Mackerel, the Cero Mackerel—both medium-sized scombroids, that may weigh up to 10 pounds—the smaller Atlantic and Chub Mackerel (4 pounds), and the huge King Mackerel, that may weigh up to 100 pounds. Also among the Scombroidae are: the Little Tuna, the Albacore, Skipjack Tuna, Blackfin Tuna, and Yellowfin Tuna. These range in weight from 20 to 265 pounds. The giant of the tuna is the Bluefin Tuna, a commercially important fish and gamefish that has reached recorded weights greater than 1600 pounds (see montage of Scombroid fish).

Scombroid fish have a rich, sometimes dark, oily flesh that many consider an excellent food. The problem is that the flesh is very rich in the amino acid histidine, and therein lies the problem. Certain bacteria such as *Proteus morganii* normally live on the surface of these fish. In cold water the bacterial population is maintained at a constant and harmless level, but if a mackerel or tuna is caught and left unrefrigerated for any length of time, the bacterial population explodes. Under optimum conditions, bacteria can reproduce every 20 minutes. These bacteria contain enzymes which act on histidine and rapidly convert it into two potent biologically active substances, histamine and another histamine-like substance, saurine. Saurine is probably the major toxin. Both act on smooth muscle of blood vessels, producing severe allergic symptoms and in some cases anaphylactic shock (see p. 114) and death. Healthy fish contains less than 0.1 milligrams of histamine, but fish unrefrigerated for twelve hours will contain a thousand times this amount.

**Distribution:** Mackerel and tuna range from Labrador, Newfoundland, Nova Scotia and the Gulf of Maine southward all the way to Brazil.

**Symptoms:** Bacterial contaminated scombroid fish appear normal and have no odor and they may even taste fine. However, sometimes spoiled fish will have a taste that has been described as pungent or peppery, which will be a warning not to eat the fish. Symptoms may appear within minutes after eating contaminated fish or may not appear until hours later. They include blistering of the mouth, loss of appetite, heachache; severe reddening (erythema) of the face, neck, and upper body, followed by hives; and spasm of the bronchial tubes with wheezing. Sometimes the victim will feel dizzy, vomit, and have abdominal cramps and diarrhea. In severe cases, when a sensitive individual has eaten a large amount of spoiled fish, the onset is sooner and the symptoms more severe. Usually within 16 hours the victim is recovered; deaths are exceedingly rare, but have been reported. Scombroid poisoning is often misdiagnosed as fish allergy.

**Prevention and Control:** Never leave mackerel or tuna in the sun or unrefrigerated for any length of time. Never eat such fish. If the fish has a peppery taste, don't eat it. The toxin is not inactivated by canning or cooking.

**First Aid:** Once symptoms start, the victim may vomit. If he doesn't, induce vomiting to remove any remaining poisoned fish out of the stomach. If you have non-prescription antihistamine pills available, give two or three times the recommended dosage.

**Medical Treatment:** Evacuate stomach with gastric lavage if the patient hasn't vomited. If respiratory problems develop, maintain adequate air way and be alert for anaphylactic shock. Usually antihistamines such as diphenhydramine (Benadryl) will control the symptoms, but if bronchospasm occurs, use sympathomimetics (adrenalin).

## BONY FISHES DANGEROUS TO EAT
## Puffer Fishes (61% ☠ )

The families Tetraodontidae and Lagocephalidae, the puffer fishes, have in their internal organs, liver, ovaries, and roe (eggs) one of the most deadly biotoxins known to man, tetrodotoxin. The first reference to this potent toxin goes back almost 4500 years, when the Egyptian Pharoh, Ti, died from puffer fish intoxication; more recently, Ian Fleming's James Bond was almost done in by a Soviet agent equipped with a retractable knife in her shoe. The knife was coated with tetrodotoxin. The deadly Japanese Globe Fish and fugu, both considered delicacies, require cooking by licensed chefs; even then there are as many as 20 deaths each year due to eating these fish. This toxin is also found in some tree frogs, salamanders, some octopus, and some venomous fish of the family Scorpionidae.

  Puffer fishes get their name from their unique ability to take in large amounts of water or air, thus inflating themselves to balloon-like shapes. On the Pacific West Coast of the United States,

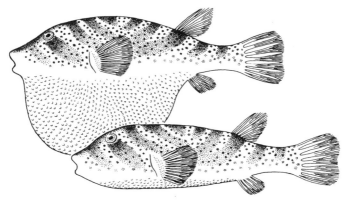

Gulf Puffer

*Spheroides annulatus*, *S. lobatus*, and *T. cutcutia* are found off Southern California. On the Atlantic side, the porcupine fish, *Diodon hystrix*, and the puffers, *S. scleratus*, *S. spengtera*, *S. maculatus*, and *T. cutcutica*, are found in the Gulf of Mexico, the Caribbean, and in Florida waters.

**Prevention and Control:** Don't eat puffer or porcupine fish. NEVER EAT LIVER, GONADS, VISCERA, OR ROE, PARTICULARLY AT BREEDING SEASON.

**Symptoms of Puffer Fish Poisoning:** There is a rapid onset of dizziness and weakness within a few minutes. Within an hour the victim may turn pale and vomit. One very distinctive symptom is a prickling or tingling sensation around the mouth, lips, tongue, and throat. As more of the nerve toxin is absorbed, this sensation can spread to the fingers and toes, and then the victim may feel numb all over. In severe poisoning there is a progressive muscular weakness and paralysis. Paralysis of rib and diaphragm muscles causes respiratory failure and death within six to 24 hours. See Poisonous Tree Frog (p. 14) and Poisonous Salamanders (p. 12) for more details.

**First Aid:** None.

**Medical Treatment:** No antidote for the poison; supportive therapy. See p. 13 for Salamander poisons.

## REPTILES DANGEROUS TO EAT
## Marine Turtles (Rarely ☠ )

Marine turtles are reptiles found mainly in subtropical oceans on both coasts of the Americas. There are two families, the Cheloniidae and the Dermochelyidae. Although they are air-breathing, they can remain under water for long periods of time. Their size is impressive, and 100-pounders are usual, except for Leatherback Turtles, whose normal weight range is from 700 to 1600 pounds. Although certain turtles are commonly accepted as edible, some of them—notably the Green Turtle—even being considered to be delicacies, they can sometimes be poisonous. Particularly dangerous is turtle liver, and in the western Indo-Pacific there are episodes in which previously edible turtles become extremely toxic. According to Dr. Halstead, 44 percent of such victims of turtle poisoning die from liver or kidney damage. Off the American coasts, turtle poisoning is rare, but the edible Hawksbill turtle, the Leatherback turtle, and very rarely the Green turtle can be poisonous.

The five species of sea turtles are shown on page 11. They include: the Leatherback (*Dermochelys coriacea*), Kemp's Ridley Turtle (*Lepidochelys kempi*), the Hawksbill (*Eretmochelys imbricata*), the Loggerhead (*Caretta caretta*), and the Green turtle (*Chelonia mydas*).

**Distribution:** All tropical and subtropical seas; only occasionally in temperate waters of both coasts.

**Symptoms of Poisoning:** Hours to days after eating a poisonous turtle, there is nausea, diarrhea, vomiting, cramps, burning sensation of mouth, lips, throat; the breath smells, and the tongue is first coated and swollen and then blistered. If poisoning is severe, lethargy sets in; the worst sign is if the victim becomes so sleepy that it is hard to keep him awake.

**Prevention:** Never eat turtle liver. Check with local fishermen who are knowledgeable about what is safe.

**First Aid:** None known; the victims usually vomit anyway.

**Medical treatment:** See ciguatera poisoning.

Leatherback
Turtle

Hawksbill
Turtle

Green
Turtle

Kemp's Ridley
Turtle

Loggerhead
Turtle

## Poisonous Salamanders (*Taricha*)( ☠ )

Salamanders are amphibians of the order Caudata. Throughout their lives they have a tail, and usually four legs—although there are a few legless species. Their feet usually have four unclawed toes, and their skin is usually smooth and moist. Salamanders have no external ear opening and in general are small, slow, and secretive. Two species are endowed with skin glands that produce an extremely deadly secretion, tetrodotoxin, which is also found in 40 different species of poisonous puffer fishes. This toxin acts on the nervous system, interfering with the movement of sodium ions across the cell membrane, a process essential for nerve cell function. The two poisonous species, found only on the west coast of the United States, are *Taricha granulosa*, the Oregon Rough-Skinned Newt, and *Taricha torosa*, the California Newt. The Oregon Newt is about two and a half to three and a half inches long, and has dark lower eyelids. Its rough upperside is usually dark brown, and its underside red-orange to yellow. The California Newt is similar in size, has light-colored lower eyelids and larger eyes, and is lighter brown, with less contrast in color between the back and belly.

**Distribution:** *T. granulosa* ranges from coastal southeastern Alaska down the west coast to Santa Cruz, California, on the west slope of the Cascades, and in the foothills of the Sierra Nevada in Colorado and Montana. *T. torosa* is found in California from Mendocino to San Diego County on the west slope of the Sierra Nevada. Both newts are found from sea level to five thousand feet or more.

**Habitat:** Ponds and streams, or in the dry season under logs and stones, usually active by day on overcast days.

**Poisoning Symptoms:** The poison is a a milky secretion secreted from skin glands in the tail region. A ten-gram newt contains about 250 micrograms of toxin, enough to kill a grown man. The toxin is 1250 times more potent than cyanide. There are two recorded human deaths, the most recent (1981), reported in the Journal of the American Medical Association, involved a 29-year-old inebriated camper who swallowed a 20-cm Oregon newt and was dead from cardiac arrest eight hours later. His lips were tingling within ten minutes, and he complained of numbness and weakness; eventually he collapsed. Six hours later in the hospital, vigorous attempts were made to resuscitate him, but they failed (see also puffer fish poisoning, p. 8). There are also several reports of pets dying after mouthing these salamanders.

**Prevention and Control:** If you pick up one of these poisonous salamanders, wash hands vigorously; do not rub eyes. Do not put in mouth even if drunk. Teach children not to put things in their mouths. Watch your pets.

**First Aid:** Empty stomach as soon after ingestion as possible. Vomiting could be the difference between life and death.

**Medical Treatment:** Induce vomiting to remove stomach contents, sulfate for muscle pain. Be prepared to provide respiratory support and also be prepared to treat for shock and Arrhythmias.

## Poisonous Newts (Neopthalmidae)( ☠ )

Eastern newts of the genus *Notophthalamus* are distinctly different from their western relatives in that they are more colorful, boasting spots, dots, or stripes. There are three Eastern Newts found in many quiet ponds, streams, and swamps. Larvae lose their gills by late summer, and become thick rough-skinned red efts. The skin of these efts, particularly on the back, contains poison secreting glands. This toxin is a potent nerve poison called tetrodotoxin or batrachotoxin and is similar, if not identical to the toxin of the Western Newts.

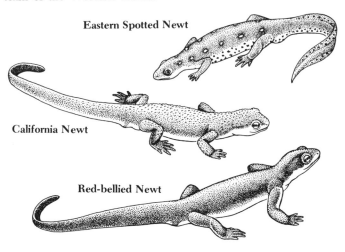

Eastern Spotted Newt

California Newt

Red-bellied Newt

The most common is the widely distributed Eastern newt, *Notophthalamus vividescens*, which as an adult is yellow to olive-brown above and yellow below and has many black dots and some dark-edged red spots. The efts are cinnamon red above and yellow or orange below. When threatened, they arch their tails to warn predators of their poisonous potential.

**Symptoms:** There are no published reports of human poisoning, but a personal communication from Dr. Arthur Echenacht suggests that care should be exercised in handling or dissecting these newts. It can be assumed that if they were eaten the results could be as fatal as the two cases involving human deaths from ingesting Western Newts.

**Prevention:** Handle with caution, preferably with gloves. Keep them away from children, who put all kinds of things in their mouths.

## Poisonous Tree Frogs (Dendrobatidae) ( ☠ )

In southern Central America, ranging down into South America, dwell a variety of small, colorful, neotropical tree frogs belonging to the family Dendrobatidae. They are diurnal terrestrial frogs often found in the vicinity of streams. They have extraordinary color patterns which are usually dark tone with spots, splotches or streaks of bright pink, yellow, green, red, orange, and even blue color patches. These gaudy colors serve a real function, that of advertising to any predator that eating one will most certainly be fatal. Even voracious frog-eating bats will veer away from one of these tiny denizens of the forest. These frogs also produce an incessant harsh chirping to announce their territory in an aggressive way. However, the most important feature of these frogs is the variety of extremely potent toxins they secrete.

**Poisonous Tree Frog**

The Dendrobatidae have also been called "the poison dart frog" because the Choco Indians of Western Colombia learned that toasting the frog over a fire caused the frog to secrete a poison that they could use with deadly effect on their blow-pipe darts. One of these darts easily has enough poison to kill a full-grown man, and a single frog secretes enough poison to load three dozen darts.

These frogs secrete several different poisons. One batrachotoxin is identical to the poison of the deadly stone fish and the California Newt. It is an extremely potent nerve poison that alters the movement of sodium ions in the nerve and muscle cells, a movement which is necessary for normal nerve and muscle function. It is one of the most potent biotoxins, and its effects seem to be almost irreversible; consequently, no antidote is known. Batrachotoxin is 25 times more potent than the arrow poison, curare, and five thousand times more potent than cyanide. It is also 10 times more powerful than the toxin secreted by the Japanese Globe Fish, one of the world's most poisonous animals. The frogs also contain pulmitiotoxins and histriocotoxins, both nerve poisons we do not know much about.

The frogs can secrete the toxin when stressed, and if you handle one of these and happen to brush your nose, you will have the sniffles and swollen runny nasal mucus membranes for two or three days. Some tree frogs if handled can cause a severe inflammation of the skin. (**Plates 15, 16, and 17.**)

**Distribution:** Columbia, Panama, the southern part of Central America, ranging down into South America.

**Prevention and Control:** Although they are beautiful, leave them alone. Actually, going into their domain puts you at great risk from both left-wing terrorists and equally unstable government troops, both of which are far more deadly than the little frogs.

**First Aid:** None.

**Medical Treatment:** Treat symptomatically; try prayer.

# Poisonous Toads (Bufonidae)
*Dangerous to Pets*

The only genus of toad in the region covered by this book is the genus *Bufo*. There are 18 different species, and two, the Giant Marine Toad (*Bufo marinus*), and the Colorado River Toad (*Bufo alvarius*), are capable of producing severe and possibly even lethal

**Giant Marine Toad**

effects. Toads are rough-skinned, squat, rather plump amphibians whose major identification marks are horizontal pupils and enlarged massive parotid glands that appear as bulging protuberances behind the eye. Although they do not cause warts as is popularly believed, all toads can secrete a poison from their parotid glands, and if this white milky toxin is inadvertently brought into contact with the mouth or eyes it can cause severe inflammation. The secretion is a protective one, and survivors who have mouthed one of the large poisonous toads will never again attack one. Deaths to dogs and cats have been frequently reported following mouthing of Marine or Colorado River toads.

*Bufo marinus* is a giant among toads, reaching lengths of 22 cm while *Bufo alvaria* is somewhat smaller, up to 17 cm. Both are nocturnal predators capable of surviving temperature ranges from 5° to 40° Celsius. Because they eat many types of insects, the Giant Marine Toad has been introduced into a number of areas for biological control of pests such as the sugar cane beetle. Unfortunately, they are prolific breeders and have multiplied to the point where they upset the local ecological balance, and in some areas there is a bounty on them. They are olive green to dark brown in color, and their bellies are cream-colored. (**Plate 18.**)

**Habitat and Distribution:** *B. marinus* was originally found from southern Texas southward all the way to Argentina, but in recent years has been introduced into Southern Florida, Puerto Rico, the West Indies, and Hawaii. They are terrestrial, preferring humid areas that offer good cover. During breeding (they breed year round) they can be found near standing water: ponds, streams, canals, and ditches.

**Toad Toxin and Its Symptoms:** Toad toxin contains several components, including a digitalis-like secretion, bufagin, and a centrally active substance, bufotenin. One milligram per kilogram of body weight will kill a dog or cat. Symptoms occur quickly after mouthing a toad. The animal starts frothy salivation, paws at the mouth, shakes his head, whines in apparent pain, vomits, and becomes uncoordinated. The heart rate and pulse accelerate, as does the rate of respiration. This may be followed by convulsions in about 30 minutes, coma, and death, which is usually due to respiratory failure. Many dogs, about 70 percent, recover within two hours after exposure. Accidental contact of bufotoxin on the eyes produces stinging, burning sensations, excruciating pain, and even temporary blindness. If it is on your hands and gets in your mouth or nasal passages, it can cause stinging, burning, and then numbing sensations.

**First Aid:** Since the poison is potentially lethal and is dependent on the amount taken, the first thing to do is wash out the dog's mouth with water while the animal lies on its side, and then get the dog to a veterinarian as quickly as possible.

**Prevention and Control:** Keep pets on a leash, away from toads. Teach children not to pick them up or put them in their mouths. If you touch one of the poisonous toads, immediately wash your hands thoroughly and avoid rubbing your eyes.

## Shellfish Dangerous to Eat ( ☠ )

Molluscs—clams, oysters, scallops, and mussels—belong to the class Pelycypoda. All have two shells, called valves, and all are bottom dwellers that are filter feeders, that is, they suck in ocean water and its contents, which then passes over the bivalves' gills, where suspended matter is trapped and passed into the digestive system. Such filter feeders have the capacity to accumulate and concentrate a variety of substances which in sea water are so dilute that they have little or no effect. There have been recorded cases of poisoning (with beryllium) (a toxic metal) in bivalves collected in beryllium-polluted waters. Infectious hepatitis has been caused by eating raw clams and oysters collected in areas polluted by sewage runoff. Another problem with such shellfish is that some people are very allergic to them. A fourth problem is that unrefrigerated shellfish spoil extremely rapidly due to bacterial growth, a fact recognized by the dietary laws of the Old Testament, which bans the eating of seafood that doesn't have scales. Ingestion of bacterial toxins in spoiled shellfish produces severe gastointestinal symptoms. Finally, bivalves have the capacity to concentrate, to lethal levels, red-tide organisms called dinoflagellates, which periodically have population explosions.

The concentrated poison, called saxiton, is a very potent nerve poison, and eating shellfish exposed to these dinoflagellates produces "paralytic shellfish poisoning." Each of these types of poisoning will be dealt with separately.

**Allergic Reactions to Shellfish:** Individuals sensitive to the proteins in bivalves vary remarkably in sensitivity, but sensitive individuals know it soon enough. Symptoms may begin 30 minutes to several hours after ingesting the bivalve. Of course, the greater the quantity eaten, the more severe the symptoms. The symptoms include itchy hives; reddening and swelling of the skin, which usually starts in the head and neck and then spreads to the rest of the body; eyelids can swell, the lips get puffy, and even the fingers can swell. Heartburn, headache, and nausea sometimes are also experienced. The shellfish proteins are apparently one of the more potent allergens, and in some cases swelling of the throat, tongue, and bronchial tubes can produce respiratory problems severe enough to kill the victim. While such deaths are rare, a few have been recorded.

**Prevention:** Allergic individuals sensitized to shellfish proteins should avoid them.

**Medical Treatment:** Antihistamines and in severe cases treat for anaphylaxis (see p. 115).

**Bacterially Contaminated Shellfish:** Several hours (eight to twelve) after eating spoiled shellfish contaminated with bacterial toxins, symptoms which have their major manifestations on the gastrointestinal tract appear. The onset is felt by queasiness and nausea, which is closely followed by vomiting, abdominal cramps that can be quite painful, and then diarrhea. The gastrointestinal upsets will usually subside after a day or two.

**Prevention:** Eat only shellfish collected from approved areas. Avoid collecting grounds near runoffs which might contain sewage. Don't eat shellfish that are not tightly closed before cooking. Do not eat shellfish that smell bad.

**First Aid:** None.

**Medical Treatment:** Symptomatic; see physician, rest. You won't feel too energetic anyway. Prevent dehydration.

## Paralytic Shellfish Poisoning (PSP) (1 to 10% ☠ )

Periodically, oceanic blooms of red-tide dinoflagellates occur on both coasts of North America and the Caribbean. Outbreaks of paralytic shellfish poisoning have been reported from the Aleutian

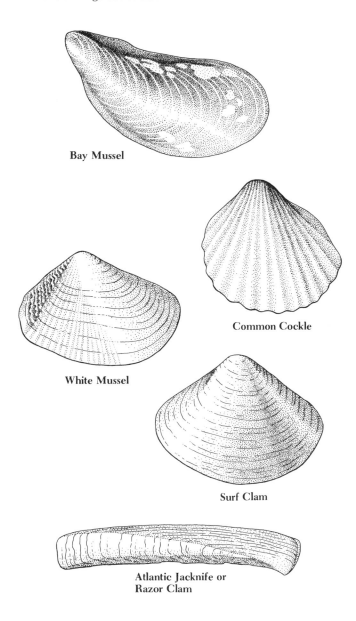

**Bay Mussel**

**Common Cockle**

**White Mussel**

**Surf Clam**

**Atlantic Jacknife or
Razor Clam**

Islands in Alaska, British Columbia, Oregon, and off the California coast southward to Baja, California; on the Atlantic coast from Canada to Florida and the West Indies, as well as the Gulf of Mexico, including Florida's west coast. There are different species of dinoflagellates involved, and there might be slight variations in toxicity. All types of bivalves have been implicated, including tiny Donax, razor clams, soft-shell clams, oysters, hard-shell clams, and mussels. The toxic substance, saxitoxin, derives its name from the genus *Saxidomus* but is similar in all species of bivalves. It is a potent nerve poison, and in cases of severe poisoning, 10 to 25 percent fatalities have been reported. Fortunately, local public health services are alert to red-tide blooms, and when one occurs shellfish beds are closed and collecting and sale are banned. In 1980, over a hundred cases of PSP were recorded in the United States, and three of them were lethal.

**Symptoms:** Within half an hour after ingesting red-tide-contaminated shellfish, a tingling, numbness, or burning sensation is felt on the lips, tongue, and mouth. These sensations spread, first over the face and head to the neck, and then to the fingers and toes. As more nerves are affected, speech may become incoherent and muscle coordination impaired to the point that the victim looks drunk. Accompanying the loss of coordination there is dizziness and loss of balance. Tightness is experienced in the throat and chest. It hurts to breath deeply. The victim feels weak, sweats, salivates, and often experiences nausea and vomiting. Reflexes disappear and in severe cases* of poisoning, the symptoms progress and 10 to 20 percent of such victims die of respiratory paralysis about eight or so hours after ingestion. Overall lethality figures are more commonly 1 to 10 percent. If the victim of paralytic shellfish poisoning survives the acute phase, lasting about ten hours, the promise of full recovery (in time) is good.

It is interesting that another form of fish poisoning which causes quite a few deaths, ciguatera poisoning, has only recently been attributed to another dinoflagellate.

**Prevention and Control:** Collect shellfish only from approved areas. Check with local shellfishermen.

**Medical Treatment:** Similar to that of ciguatera (see p. 5).

*NOTE: Severity is determined by magnitude of symptoms.

# PART II

# *Animals That Bite*

### Dogs (*Canis*): ☠ 10 per year

Dogs are all descendants of ancient wild canines that were domesticated and selectively bred, starting about 60,000 years ago. As their name implies, they possess a pair of long sharp canine teeth in both upper and lower jaws, and have powerful muscles controlling these jaws. They are not only used as pets but work to herd and protect other domestic animals and protect homes and property. Behaviorally they exhibit a range of responses from friendly to very aggressive attack behavior. The exact number of dogs in the United States is not known, but is estimated to be about thirty million. Their population is responsible for more than 600,000 reported dog bites per year (89.1 percent of all bite wounds). Thus, dogs are clearly the most common of biting animals for which we have statistics. Of those 600,000 bites, there were eleven fatalities in the latest year for which data could be found (1974–1975). It is appropriate that the designation "canine teeth" (Latin for "dog teeth") in mammals should designate the prominent stabbing teeth in both upper and lower jaws.

**Dog**

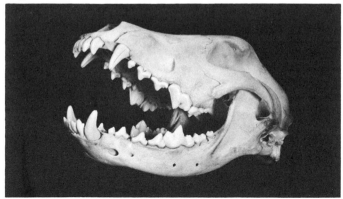

Despite popular myths, North American wolves have not been involved in attacks on humans. Our other wild canine, the coyote, an intelligent, highly adaptable smaller cousin to the wolf, has been increasingly reported in lightly populated areas and is responsible for many attacks on domestic animals. A coyote if cornered will bite, as will any frightened animal. In 1981 a child in California was killed by a coyote.

**Prevention and Control:** Do not pet strange dogs. Do not startle, irritate, or play too roughly even with pet dogs. Be particularly attentive to signs warning "attack dog" or "dangerous dog." Be careful of very large dogs, such as Great Danes, Saint Bernards, Boxers, Police Dogs, or Dobermans, since all are strong enough to kill with their powerful jaws and long, sharp canine teeth. Do not run away when approached, as this is the surest way to get bitten.

**Treatment:** Any dog that bites a human must be checked for rabies. Dogs are still the most usual source of rabies in humans, and while there are fewer than a thousand rabid dogs reported annually in the United States, their bites may be responsible for five or six cases of human rabies per year (see p. 32 for a discussion on rabies). Dog bites can be the source of several kinds of infection, and while less dangerous than human bites, control of infection is critical. The detailed protocols for symptoms, first aid, and medical treatment for bites is covered in the following material, which focuses on human bites. This text will not consider other bacterial, viral, fungal, and parasitic diseases that dogs can transmit to humans.

## Cats: (*Felis*) Bite and Scratch

Cats are also carnivores, and the large American cats—Jaguar, Puma, Bobcat—although capable of inflicting serious or even lethal wounds on humans, are so shy and secretive in their behavior that human contact is extremely rare. Domestic cats cause 4.6 percent of all reported bite wounds. They exist in great numbers, probably more than dogs, and there may be more than forty million cats in the United States. Cats are remarkably independent, are marvelous bird catchers, and can learn to kill rats and mice. Cats are equipped with retractable, very sharp, pointed claws under which bits of decaying flesh can serve as culture media for a number of bacteria and virus. A cat scratch,

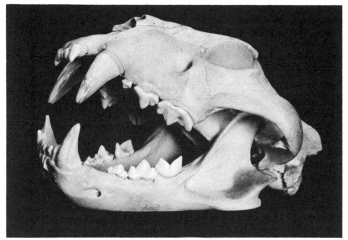

Cat

thus, can cause a variety of infections, and there is a specific viral disease called Cat Scratch Fever which can be transmitted by either cat bites or scratches. Cats can also carry rabies, and about 300 rabid cats are found each year.

Cat Scratch Fever is probably caused by viral or chlamydial type bacteria. It occurs sporadically, often as a small epidemic, and may be endemic (always present) in places like Toronto, Canada, or New York City. Symptoms may appear seven to 20 days after a scratch or bite and affect the lymphatics, causing enlarged nodes, elevated lymphocytes, pustules, and papules, and areas of reddening around the scratch. The glands are painful, and the fever usually short-lasting; the recovery may take several weeks but is spontaneous. Most cases are found in children. In temperate areas, fall and winter are the seasons for cat scratch disease, while in warmer climates it occurs year round. Best control is to prevent being scratched by a cat. If you are bitten or scratched by a cat, follow first aid measures described in section on human bites.

## Human Bites (*Homo sapiens*)

Man's mouth is a powerful weapon capable of producing mutilation of, and infection to, human tissue. The flora of the human mouth is diverse, and a neglected bite wound can have serious complications.

In 1977 a study was undertaken in New York City and the surrounding area in an attempt to learn more about the epidemiologic distribution of human bites. It was found that human bites are the third most common type of bite wound, occurring in 3.6 percent of all bite cases. Dog, cat and rodent bites account for 89.1 percent, 4.6 percent, and 2.2 percent of all bite wounds respectively. The reasons for one person biting another fall into two categories: aggressive acts, which account for 72.6 percent of all bites and non-aggressive acts, which make up the remaining 27.4 percent. Aggressive acts include fighting (59.9 percent), police arrests (8.4 percent), and mugging (4.3 percent), while non-aggressive acts include playing (12.1 percent), school activity (4.5 percent), medical or dental treatment (3.2 percent), sexual (0.4 percent), and miscellaneous (7.1 percent). The distribution of these bites was 61.5 percent to the arms, 14.9 percent to the head and neck, 11.5 percent to the thorax and abdomen, 8.6 percent to "unknown parts," and 3.7 percent to the lower extremities. The incidence of bites is lowest in January and February and increases through the spring to a peak during the summer. Fighting is an important factor in explaining the seasonal variation in the occurrence of bites, as it is in accounting for the four-to-one male-to-female bite ratio.

**Effects of Bites (Humans and Other Animals):** Infection is a major problem in all types of bites, but human bites are particularly dangerous because of the diversity and number of bacteria found in the human mouth and saliva. Human saliva may contain as many as one hundred million bacteria per milliliter, and over 42 species of bacteria have been isolated. Of these 42 species, both aerobic and anaerobic organisms are represented. It would seem at first that since these bacteria are already present in humans they should present no major problem; this is untrue. The bacteria of the mouth present no danger only in the undamaged oral cavity, but when they are introduced into the tissues and into the blood from a bite wound, infection becomes a major threat. In fact, the act of biting flesh, or punching a tooth into flesh actually inoculates saliva and bacteria deep into the tissues, thereby worsening their threat. The most frequently encountered in severe infections are the staphylococcus and streptococcus. The fungus *Actinomyces bovis* is also common in the mouth. In contrast, a dog's saliva, which most people consider to be more harmful than human saliva, normally contains only seven organisms, and thus is much less dangerous than human saliva. The microorganisms of the mouth invade the blood and tissues and cause infection, as would other microbial invasions. As mentioned earlier, there is the added severity of infection from bites, because the microorganisms are sometimes inoculated deep into the flesh, thereby allowing them to thrive deep inside the skin.

In addition to bacterial infection from bite wounds, viral diseases can also be passed from one person to another by biting, for example Hepatitis "B" virus (HBV).

More often than dog bites, human bites are left unattended for days, or until infection is severe. An unattended bite can result in "florid" hand infections and loss of hand function. According to Homer House, M.D., and Donald Morris, M.D., human bites are known to cause "progressive foul infections that have been difficult to treat once established."

There are numerous examples in the literature which list the devastating complications that can result from inadequately treated bites to the hand. These include recurrent infection, permanent joint stiffness, osteomyelitis (an infection), tetanus, and gas gangrene.


**First Aid for Bites:** The standard first aid for a human bite wound, if it is not too extensive, is to milk some blood from the wound to try and flush out as many organisms as possible, and then wash the wound with soap and water. A physician should be seen in the case of a bite wound of any severity if the skin has been broken.


**Medical Treatment for Bites:** Medical treatment of bites is diverse, and a lot of controversy surrounds the best way to treat them. Standard emergency-room procedure is to treat any laceration of incisor size to the knuckle region as caused by a bite as infected until proven otherwise. Aggressive early treatment of suspected infection is recommended. All suspected infections should be cultured. Foreign matter and damaged tissue are removed surgically. Localized pus is drained and thoroughly irrigated with saline.

Antibiotic choice and regimen of treatment is varied. Penicillin-ase-resistant anti-staphylococcal antibiotics such as dicloxicillin, oxacillin, or cephalosporin are used for early treatment and are supplemented by gentamicin in wounds showing delay in treatment or evidence of Gram-negative organisms. The duration of antibiotic treatment is varied. In addition to antibiotics, a tetanus toxoid booster should be given if the patient has not had one in the past five years.

## Bears (Ursidae) (Three fatalities per 100 Attacks) ( ☠ )

There are eight species of North American bears. These include the Grizzlies and Alaska Brown Bears, Polar Bears, and the American Black Bear. Bears are stocky, usually slow moving, large animals. They have low population densities and low rates of reproduction. Their diets vary, and they usually den over in the wintertime. Bears are not normally aggressive, but they are powerful animals capable of severely mauling or killing a full-grown human. About a hundred bear attacks on humans are recorded annually, and the vast majority could have easily been avoided had the victims used a little common sense.

## Grizzly Bears (*Ursus horribilis*): Maul, Bite (Rarely ☠ )

The term "grizzly" means grayish, although this term is misleading, since the coarse-coated grizzlies range in color from almost yellow-brown to very dark brown or black. Some bears have frosted hair tips, hence, the name "silver tip" has also been used. Dr. C. Hart Merriam of the Smithsonian Institution lists 86 variants of the species *horribilis*, and these include the Kodiaks and Alaskan Brown Bears. The species name, *horribilis*, means inspiring horror, and indeed these large bears are awesome. Weights of over 1600 pounds have been recorded, although 600 to 800 is the usual adult weight. These bears are up to four feet tall at the shoulder and may measure up to nine feet from the tip of the nose to the tip of the short tail. They are heavy-bodied, measuring

**Grizzly Bear**

as much as eight feet around the trunk. They have very long, thick, flattened claws (thick as a man's finger at the base), up to five inches long, and although they are not as sharp-pointed as the claws of a black bear, they are capable of inflicting deadly wounds. All grizzlies have a distinctive shoulder hump when viewed in profile, due to their powerful roll of shoulder muscles. Their faces are also characteristically concave, hence, they are sometimes called dish-faced bears. Grizzlies are usually shy and slow moving, and will normally avoid humans. However, they can move at 30 miles per hour for short bursts and can go through thickets that would stop a four-wheel-drive truck. Their diet is highly varied, and an adult bear can consume up to 90 pounds of salmon in a day. They have excellent sense of smell and hearing. Grizzlies den over in the winter, may produce two cubs a year, reach maturity at eight or ten years of age, and may live to 30. Without question, these huge bears are the most powerful and potentially the most dangerous of American land mammals. (See cover photo.)

**Distribution:** Grizzlies range from Alaska and Arctic Canada southward through the Rocky Mountain states, and rarely in the mountains of northern Mexico. Their numbers have been severely depleted, and only a few hundred remain in the National Parks (Glacier, North Cascades, Yellowstone). Most grizzlies avoid humans and are found in wilderness areas.

**Human attacks:** Attacks are usually related to threatening or startling a bear, or approaching too close to a mother bear and her cubs. It has also been suggested, on the basis of two cases of women in sleeping bags being mauled, that bears are sometimes attracted to human female odors, possibly triggering a territorial or sexual response.

**Prevention:** Don't walk by salmon streams or berry patches. If you encounter a grizzly close up, don't run; back off slowly. If you have a chance climb well up in a tree, because grizzlies can't climb. They can, however, stand on their hind limbs and have a surprising reach. If you are caught, lie still. Apparently bears will leave you alone if you don't move, and it may be that bears don't like the way humans smell.

**First Aid:** Stop the bleeding, prevent shock, clean lacerations, and get to medical care as rapidly as possible. See Rabies (p. 32), Tetanus (p. 32), and general discussion of treatment of bites.

Black Bear

## Black Bears (*Evarctos americanus*) Maul, Bite (Rarely  )

Black Bears are not often black at all, but are usually some shade of brown and are therefore sometimes referred to as Cinnamon Bears. There is even one race of Black Bears in British Colombia that is white. However, most are dark brown to black, although their snouts are usually brown, and in older bears grizzled and almost white. They are medium-sized bears, usually weighing only 200 or 300 pounds, but 500-pound adults have been recorded. They measure about five feet in length and are equipped with short, curved, sharp claws that permit them to climb trees quite well. While omnivorous, eating anything from garbage to insects and berries, they will prey on deer and other animals. They are the most numerous bear, and in some areas will hang around campsites. In some national parks, these bears have become deceptively tame, but they are potentially dangerous, and in the majority of the one hundred or so bear attacks on humans per year, the Black Bear is the culprit.

**Distribution:** From Maine to Florida; Canada.

**Prevention:** Treat them with respect and avoid them. If you climb a tree they may follow; a sharp blow across the snout may discourage your pursuer.

**First Aid:** Control bleeding, prevent shock, cleanse wounds. See pages 24 and 25 for specifics.

## Polar Bears (*Thalarctos maritimus*): Maul, Bite (Rarely ☠)

Polar Bears (*Thalarctos maritimus*) are found all around the Arctic Circle from Alaska, the northern edge of Hudson Bay, and through the Canadian Arctic. Today it is estimated that no more than twelve thousand of these magnificent bears remain, and they are threatened with extinction. These large cream-colored animals are efficient hunters, mainly eating seals. They lack fear, and an adult male weighs a thousand pounds, and is five feet tall and about eight feet long. When they stand upright on their hind legs, as they often do, they can be up to twelve feet tall. Despite their size, they move with incredible grace. Their heavy white fur covers all of the body except for their charcoal-black noses. They are extremely powerful, and a single swipe of their 50-pound paws can kill a quarter-of-a-ton seal. They are superb swimmers, and on land they can run at 35 miles per hour.

Polar bears are curious and generally retiring. However, when angered they are formidable. There are well-documented reports of bear attacks on humans resulting in badly mauled or dead victims. These attacks are very rare and very often provoked. Bears in the summer are attracted to the smell of food or garbage at camp sites. You cannot scare off a big bear, and they should be avoided and left alone. Although some bears can be hunted with licenses during the hunting season, hunters should be warned not to eat polar bear liver because it contains such high concentrations of vitamin D that it disrupts calcium balance in the body and can be lethal.

**Avoidance/Control:** The best advice is not to get too close.

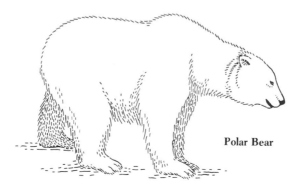

**Polar Bear**

## Bats (Chiroptera): Bite, Transmit Rabies

Bats are flying mammals widely distributed across North America. They are nocturnal hunters viewed by most humans with loathing and fear, yet this fear is largely unjustified, and the insect-eating bats (the insectivora) are beneficial to man. Only one species, whose northern limit is central Mexico, is known to attack humans with any consistency. This is the Vampire Bat, whose bite is often a source of the usually lethal rabies virus. As a matter of fact, on very rare instances even insectivorous bats can transmit this deadly virus, which makes the infected bat very aggressive and fearless of man. All 50 states have reported bat bites on humans, and it is mandatory that if you have been bitten by a bat or any wild or even domesticated mammal that you should immediately see a physician.

One other problem associated with bats, particularly those of the tropics and sub-tropical areas (Central America and the Carribean) is a health hazard in exploring bat caves. A significant number of bats are host to a highly contagious fungus, and the spores from this fungus are found in bat droppings (guano). Inhaling airborne spores in a bat cave or roosting area can produce severe pneumonia-like symptoms. Fortunately, many people have developed an immunity to histoplasmosis by previous exposure to infected animal guano. Nevertheless, if you plan to do some spelunking (exploring caves) in the tropics, you should have a respiratory mask. Should you develop pneumonia-like symptoms after cave exploring, you should call your physician and inform him about possible exposure to histoplasmosis.

**Vampire Bat**

## Vampire Bats (Demodontidae): Bite, Eat Blood, Transmit Rabies

The commonest species of Vampire Bat is *Desmodus rotundus.* Like all blood-eating (hematophagus) bats, this brown nocturnal hunter is found only in areas where the winter temperature never drops below 10° C. The average vampire only weighs from 30 to 50 grams (a nickel weighs five grams), yet it can feed on prey thousands of times larger than itself. The usual prey is cattle, and in Central and South America literally hundreds of thousands of cattle have died from vampire-bite-transmitted rabies. Human attacks have been recorded for over three thousand years, but in general these attacks are rare. The last major outbreak of vampire-transmitted rabies in humans occurred in Costa Rica in 1936, when 89 humans died from paralytic rabies.

**Habitat and Distribution:** Vampires range from Central Mexico southward across Panama into South America. They tend to be gregarious, nesting in clusters inside of hollow trees. Hunting is usually specific for cattle, with the greatest incidence of bites on moonless nights; however, pregnant females, whose need for protein is greater, are less specific in their choice of prey and will attack exposed humans. The Bite: Vampires use a good sense of vision and smell to locate prey. Their approach is stealthy and they are very agile, being able to walk, run, hop, and jump. They will bite any exposed area, and their eight razor-sharp teeth produce a bite that is so delicate that it can't be felt. The wound, a 3 mm bite, bleeds profusely because bat saliva contains three potent substances which inhibit the blood clotting mechanism. A bat usually consumes 15 ml of blood a day and can increase its fasting weight by 40 percent in one eating session. Many vampires (30 to 50 percent of them during peak seasons) carry rabies virus in their saliva, and this is the source of human infection. Rabies infections in bats follows a two to three-year cycle, and incidence is highest in the wet season. Even after feeding has ceased and the vampire bat departs, the wound still continues to bleed profusely because of the anticoagulant in the saliva.

**Prevention:** Modern well-netted tents or good mosquito netting will act as physical barriers to vampires. Unfortunately, many small hotels and inns in Central America lack window screens, which also keep vampires out.

## Rabies (Possible from All Biting Animals) (Untreated 100% ☠️ )

**Symptoms:** The symptoms of rabies infection have been in the literature since 1800 B.C., and few people are known to have recovered from this disease once clinical symptoms have appeared. The causative agent associated with the saliva is a bullet-shaped virus which enters through the wound, penetrates nerve endings, migrates within the nerve cells to the spinal cord, and from there to the brain. During this whole time, which may take weeks to months, the virus multiplies. From the brain, the virus moves out in all the nerves including those to the salivary glands, where the virus continues to multiply. The early symptoms include: a change in disposition, restlessness, and anxiety; this is followed by a stage of fury and aggressiveness. Dogs and other animals in this stage lose fear and bite anything nearby. As the disease progresses, the lower jaw droops, there is extensive frothy salivation, and there develops an inability to drink, possibly because it is so painful to swallow. Thus, hydrophobia, fear of water, is a common symptom. In the final stages of the disease, motor paralysis begins and movement becomes uncoordinated, as in severe alcoholic states. The cause of death is always respiratory failure due to paralysis of the muscles involved in breathing.

**First Aid:** None! If bitten by any wild warm-blooded animal (squirrels, skunks, foxes, bats) or domesticated animal (cats or dogs), see your physician immediately. Successful treatment must begin as soon as possible.

**Medical Treatment:** Until recently treatment consisted of 14 to 21 painful injections. Every year over a million people have been treated, and it is estimated that at least 30,000 people are treated annually in the United States. A new treatment involving only four to six inoculations has been perfected, and with this new vaccine there are relatively few side effects. Once again the treatment MUST be started within a short time of being bitten.

## Tetanus (Possible from All Biting Animals)

Tetanus can also occur from improperly cleaned, closed wounds. It is caused by the anaerobic bacterium *Clostridium tetani*, which secretes tetanus toxin. This toxin mainly effects the nervous system. The incubation period ranges from four to 21 days. Symptoms include headache, stiffness of the jaw (lockjaw), muscle spasms, and rapid pulse. Death is usually a result of respiratory arrest. This disease can be prevented by proper surgical therapy of wounds and passive or active immunization. However, if the clinical tetanus appears hyperimmune, human tetanus anti-toxin, muscle relaxants, and antibiotics should be given.

## BONY FISHES THAT BITE
## Barracuda (*Sphyraena*): Bite, Very Dangerous to Eat

There are seven species of barracuda (*Sphyraena*) found off the coast of North and Central America. The most important of these are the Great Barracuda, *S. barracuda*, of the Atlantic coast and the Silver Barracuda, *S. argentea*, of the Pacific coast. These fish, often called "Tigers of the Sea," are powerful, swift, fearsome predators with long, slender, muscular bodies and large pointed heads. Their large mouths and jutting lower jaw are lined with awesome razor-sharp pointed teeth, some as long as three-quarters of an inch. The longer teeth are for seizing their prey, smaller fish, and the dagger-like smaller backward curving teeth are mainly used for cutting or shredding. Given this armament, the barracuda's head is its outstanding identification feature. The average great barracuda is about four feet long, but specimens almost ten feet long and weighing up to 100 pounds have been reported.

These handsome, fearless killing machines are often seen hanging almost stationary or gliding slowly in the water, but they

**Great Barracuda**

are capable of swift speeds when they attack. They are curious and rarely attack humans, and when they do it is usually one swift bite, after which they swim away. The bite can tear out a considerable hunk of flesh and usually produces a clean straight wound, unlike that inflicted by a shark. Although barracuda bites are rare and are seldom fatal, eating a Great Barracuda can be very dangerous, because these fish are the major cause of ciguatera poisoning (see p. 1). In one recent episode (1982) at Bimini Island, fifteen sailors were hospitalized, several in critical condition, after eating a Great Barracuda they caught. Do not eat any barracuda over three pounds in weight.

**Distribution:** Tropical Atlantic and Pacific Oceans. Usually from South Carolina into the Caribbean, although some have been reported as far north as Massachusetts. On the Pacific Coast from California south to Panama. (**Plate 25.**)

**Prevention and Control:** It has been reported that they are attracted to bright colors. If you see Great Barracuda when snorkeling or scuba diving, move slowly away, since barracuda usually circle you for a long time before making their move. Small barracuda are harmless (and good to eat) and will often swim alongside you. Attacks sometimes occur in murky waters, or when one of these pugnacious predators has been speared. DO NOT EAT LARGE BARRACUDAS!

**First Aid:** The first step is to control blood loss. It can cause the victim to go into shock and die. Use a tourniquet only if absolutely necessary. Use a compression bandage on oozing wounds. Get the patient to a physician.

**Medical Treatment:** Control blood loss; clean the wound, being alert for foreign material; be alert for shock, infection.

# Moray Eels (Muraenidae): Bite, Very Dangerous to Eat

Moray Eels (Muraenidae), despite their snake-like appearance and smooth leathery skin, are true bony fish. They are both beautiful and repulsive-looking, moderate-sized predators that dwell in temperate and tropical oceans. They are largely nocturnal and during the day seek out holes or crevices in the rocks or coral. Usually only their head and a bit of the body can be seen protruding from their lair. They are equipped with powerful jaw muscles, and the jaws are lined with both long and short

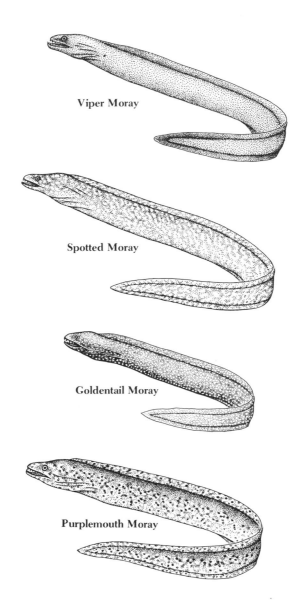

Viper Moray

Spotted Moray

Goldentail Moray

Purplemouth Moray

backward-curving teeth capable of inflicting a savage bite. They can strike with great rapidity, and according to Dr. Halstead, one of the pioneers on dangerous marine life, "they may retain their bulldog-like grip until death." You can't pull them out of their lairs, since they are quite powerful and their leathery, tough skin is not easily cut with a knife. Their skin has mucous glands; thus they are extremely slippery and impossible to grab. While they can produce jagged, potentially dangerous bites, they rarely attack humans, although any specimen over three feet in length should be viewed with great caution. The main problem with morays is that they are very often ciguatoxic, and under no circumstances should they be eaten.

**Types of American Morays:** The largest Atlantic moray, the Green Moray (*G. funebris*), reaches lengths of six feet and is actually blue, but the yellowish mucus secreted by its skin gives it a green color. The Spotted Moray, *G. moringa*, may reach lengths of four feet and is usually found in the shadows of rocky outcroppings in coral reefs. The meanest-looking moray, the Viper Moray, *E. nigricans*, has arched jaws that show some of its awesome array of teeth even when its jaws are shut. The Purple-Mouthed Moray, *G. vicinus*, is a brownish, heavily mottled and spotted four-footer whose mouth, as its name implies, is lavender or purplish in color. See page 35 for a montage showing these awesome predators. (**Plate 26.**)

**Habitat and Distribution:** Tropical or subtropical shallow ocean dwellers, most abundant and common in coral reefs, where they are found in crevices or holes.

**Green Moray Eel**

**Prevention and Control:** Never stick your hands or arms into holes or crevices. UNDER NO CIRCUMSTANCES EAT MORAY EELS; THEY ARE CIGUATOXIC.

**First Aid:** Stop bleeding, see physician.

**Medical Treatment:** Same as for barracuda bites; also ciguatera poisoning on page 5.

## Cartilaginous Fishes (Elasmobranchii): Bite, Some Dangerous to Eat

Sharks are elasmobranchs, fish whose skeletons are made up of cartilage rather than bone. They have been around in more or less the same form for well over a hundred million years, a longevity that attests to their success. These denizens of the deep are found in most oceans of the world and sometimes estuaries and river mouths. There is even one species found in Nicaragua that is a lake dweller. Over 350 species of sharks have been classified, and only ten have been reported to attack humans. Sharks range in size from 18 inches to 45 feet. The very largest, the whale shark, is actually a harmless plankton grazer. Of the species that attack humans, the real man-killer is the great white shark, which according to a recent report may reach lengths of 28 feet. According to Dr. Halstead, any shark larger than four feet should be considered dangerous.

Sharks are torpedo-shaped, streamlined, powerfully muscled hunters. They are tireless predators and are at times cannibalistic; until man came along sharks' worst enemy was probably other

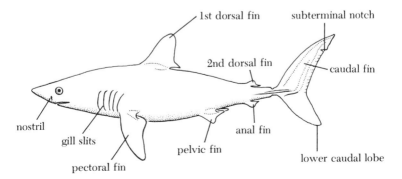

**Shark**

sharks. Only humans hunt sharks, and the shark catch in the world
is over 300,000 metric tons annually. Sharks would have to eat
about five million humans per year to reach equality. Sharks
(particularly the Mako) are hunted for sport, for food, for profit,
and out of fear. In the Orient, shark fin is considered a rare
delicacy, and many sharks are killed, relieved of their dorsal fins,
and then dumped overboard. Shark jaws are also a marketable
commodity, and so are larger shark teeth. A good set of jaws from
a very large shark can bring as much as a thousand dollars, while
thousands of small sets of jaws can be bought for as little as a dollar
apiece. Sharks' teeth are also considered collectibles, and a large
Great White has teeth 2½ inches long, while his ancestral great-
grandfather of fifty million years ago left us with fossilized five-
inch teeth.

   Sharks have a pair of expressionless eyes that are effective in
dim light, and they use vision only when close to their prey. For
long-distance location, the sharks use an extraordinary sense of
smell. They have a pair of nostrils at the snout that lead to an array
of sensors. Much of the shark's brain is utilized in analyzing
information about odors. Not only can sharks smell blood in the
water at considerable distances—hundreds of meters—but they
can also respond to secretions of distressed fish. They have an
uncanny ability to home in on such a smell, and it has been
suggested that odor may play a role in producing "mob eating" or
"feeding frenzy" that has often been seen. Sharks also can use low-
frequency sound vibrations to locate prey as far away as a hundred
meters. To do this, they use both their internal ears and the lateral

line network of sensory receptors that runs the length of the body. Actually sharks have more intelligence than previously thought, and recent experiments have shown that they can both learn and remember.

Sharks have five to seven pairs of prominent gill slits through which they breathe, and contrary to popular belief, they don't have to keep moving to breathe. Most sharks are strong swimmers that move by sideways undulations of the body and tail, which push the water back and the fish forward. Fins along the midline help in steering, and the tail or caudal fin aids in propulsion. Paired fins corresponding to our arms and legs play a role in steering and stabilizing movement. The main dorsal fin and sometimes the top of the caudal fin may sometimes be seen slicing through the water when the shark is hunting near the surface. Generally, when you see this, get out of the water (see p. 37 for main features of the shark's external anatomy).

Sharkskin contains millions of small pointed bony structures called denticles. They look like small teeth and give sharkskin a sandpaper-like quality. Indeed, brushing against a shark can take off quite a bit of skin. It is thought that these denticles also gave rise to the peculiar teeth that line the shark's jaw.

Sharks actually possess several series of teeth, and, depending on the species, there may be from five to 15 rows. Some of these rows are made up of small immature replacement teeth pointing in a reverse direction and located behind the rows of functional teeth. As functional teeth are lost, a process that continues throughout the shark's life, replacement teeth move forward to take their place. The process of replacement requires about one week, and in some species a whole series of teeth may be replaced at one time. The teeth vary in shape according to species, and tooth shape has been used as a means of identification. Some species have sharply pointed slender teeth, and others have wedge-shaped teeth with edges serrated like saw blades. The Great White has such serrated teeth, and in a large specimen they may be two and one-half inches long (see cover photo and **Plate 23**). The teeth are arranged in a more or less continuous cutting edge (see photo showing shark jaw anatomy).

## Shark Behavior

Most of the time, sharks seem to cruise along in a slow, almost sluggish, determined manner, but are capable of sudden and swift acceleration when they move to attack. Some, like the Great White, attack without warning, usually from behind. It is thought that the attack is not a form of aggressive behavior and the shark is just hungry, not angry. However, if sharks are annoyed, they exhibit a characteristic series of postures that are considered threat displays. They arch their backs, raise their heads, lower their pectoral fins, and swim in a stiff, jerky manner. A diver seeing this behavior would be well advised to get out of the water. When in this annoyed or angry state, sharks have been known to actually attack boats, and both the Great White and Mako Sharks have records as boat biters.

## Shark Attacks on Humans (10 Fatalities per 50 Attacks Worldwide per Year)

For the past three decades, the U.S. Navy and the Smithsonian Institution have been compiling a worldwide listing of shark attacks on humans. The number is surprisingly small, averaging only 28 attacks per year for the whole world. Given the limitations of reporting, perhaps twice that number occur. Despite the infrequency of such attacks, sharks are still a major object of human fear. Actually, it seems that sharks don't like the taste of human flesh, and the majority of human attacks consist of a single, albeit damaging, bite, after which the shark lets go. Actually, only about 20 percent of shark attack victims die, usually as the result of massive loss of blood.

Most shark attacks occur when water temperatures range between 70° and 85°F. Although in colder waters off both California and the East Coast, shark-caused human deaths have been reported in water temperatures below 60°F. According to Dr. Halstead, the maximum number of attacks occur in January, usually between 3 and 4 p.m. One third of all shark attack victims are skin divers. Skin divers get close to sharks, and more often than not the diver is stupid enough to have molested the shark and provoked the attack. Half of the attacks on divers occurred during spearfishing, possibly because the thrashing fish or blood in the water attracted the shark's attention. Statistics indicate that sharks prefer males to females. One report found that for each female attacked, thirteen males were attacked, but these figures may be dated, and the ratio will probably change as females increasingly engage in sports previously limited to males. Actually, in 1973 the ratio of shark attack was one female to 243 males. These numbers say a lot. Males are products of a cultural demand for "macho-type behavior," and this behavior puts males at greater risk for all dangerous creatures. It doesn't make much sense to tangle with an 18-foot hammerhead just to prove your manhood.

The shark's jaws and teeth are extraordinary. They have a

tremendous gape, and they can actually dislocate their jaws at will. One ancient ancestor to the Great White shark had a gape large enough to swallow a Volkswagen Beetle. Today's largest sharks can't do this, but they can easily swallow a 200-pound man. The jaw muscles of a shark are extremely powerful, and when the shark bites down, the force may be more than eighteen tons per square inch.

Once the shark bites its prey, it shakes its victim fiercely, tearing out large amounts of flesh and leaving a very ragged wound, which bleeds copiously.

**Prevention:** According to the U.S. Navy-supported Shark Research Panel:

1. Use your head, not your ego. Do not go into waters where sharks have been reported.
2. Don't swim alone or dive alone.
3. If spearfishing, boat your catch quickly; sharks may be attracted to the splashing and blood or distress scent in the water.
4. Leave sharks alone; don't annoy them. Even small, four-foot sharks can produce a damaging bite.
5. Avoid wearing bright, shiny, or reflecting objects.
6. Don't swim in areas where human garbage has been dumped previously.
7. If you see a shark, swim away without splashing and leave the water.
8. If attacked, fend off the shark with anything available, but be careful using your fist, since the denticles in sharkskin are so sharp and abrasive that they can take all the skin off your knuckles. Defensive efforts have had some success.*

**First Aid:** Prompt and vigorous control of bleeding by use of gauze pressure bandages. Stuff gauze into wound and hold in place very firmly with one or more Ace elastic bandages. If a large artery is severed, the blood will spurt out. In such cases, place a tourniquet between the wound and the heart. However, tourniquet use should be done only in extreme cases, and preferably by an experienced person. Massive loss of blood and tissue loss can both lead to shock, a severe drop in blood pressure, and inadequate amounts of blood reaching the vital organs. After controlling the blood loss, lay the victim down, elevate the legs slightly, and keep the victim warm. Calm and reassure the victim, and get him to medical attention as soon as possible.

*Based on recommendations of the U.S. Navy-supported Shark Research Panel.

**Medical Treatment:** Continue control of bleeding and treat for shock with I.V. fluids and whole blood. Tetanus antitoxin should be given (or a booster if subject has previously received tetanus toxoid inoculation). Antibiotic therapy is suggested. Surgical repair in hospital as needed.

## The Great White Shark: Bites, Very Dangerous ( ☠ Man-Eater)

The Mackerel Shark family (Isuridae) are considered to be man-eaters. The shark responsible for the most lethal attacks and certainly the most dangerous shark is an Isurid, the Great White (*Carcharodon charcharias*). The Great White, as its name implies, is the largest of the predatory sharks. A Great White recently caught off Portugal was 28 feet long. These sharks are relentless and efficient hunters that have been described as "savage," "aggressive" and "sinister." They often attack without warning from behind, and for such a large creature can move with surprising speed. They are torpedo-shaped, have a prominent dorsal fin, a lunate caudal fin, and a pointed snout. Each tooth has a heavily serrated cutting edge and these triangular-shaped teeth may be as much as two and a half inches long. They are composed of extremely hard material and there are reports of Great Whites biting through steel cables.

Large Great Whites may be brownish white or even "leaden white" but medium-sized Great Whites are actually dull slate-brown, slate-blue or gray. Often there is a black spot on the pectoral fins and the tips of the pectorals are usually dark tipped. The dorsal fin and caudal fin are also dark edged. (**Plate 23.**)

**Distribution:** Great Whites are found in most oceans, particularly in tropical and subtropical waters, although in the summer months they invade warmer temperate areas as far north as the

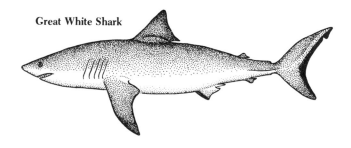

**Great White Shark**

New England coast. Fortunately they are not abundant in American waters.

**Prevention, First Aid, Medical Treatment are covered on pages 41 and 42.**

## Hammerhead Sharks (Sphyrnidae): Dangerous

One of the most readily identified families of sharks are the Sphyrnidae, whose distinctive flattened head or "bonnet" gives them the name hammerhead. While we are not sure what the functional significance of such a bizarre head shape is, it has been suggested that the head acts as an auxiliary steering apparatus. Another suggestion is that the nostrils and eyes being located at the outer edges of the hammer give this predator a sensory advantage in hunting.

In American waters there are three species of hammerheads that are potentially dangerous: the Scalloped Hammerhead (*S. lewini*), the Smooth Hammerhead (*S. zygaena*) both reaching a maximum length of about 12 feet, and the Great Hammerhead (*S. mokarran*), the largest, most dangerous member of the family, which may reach lengths of 18 feet. Human remains have been found in the stomachs of these swift, powerful predators, and there are well documented attacks on humans by large hammerheads.

**Distribution:** Hammerheads are widely distributed throughout warm and tropical oceans off the American coast and are often found in inshore, shallow, murky waters.

**Bite and Symptoms:** The shark's jaw, with its rows of cutting, tearing teeth, is an extraordinarily powerful machine. Ham-

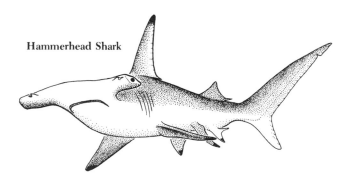

**Hammerhead Shark**

merhead attacks usually involve a single bite, which can produce a very ragged wound, often with considerable loss of flesh and sometimes massive bleeding. The tissue loss, although severe, is usually not the problem, but the blood loss can quickly lead to shock and death.

**Prevention:** Same for all shark bites, see details on p. 41.

**First Aid:** Same for all shark bites, see details on p. 41.

**Medical Treatment:** Same for all shark bites, see details on p. 42.

## The Mako or Sharp-Nosed Mackerel Shark: Dangerous

One member of the family Isuridae that has a very bad reputation is the Mako Shark (*Isurus oxyrinchus rafinesque*). Smaller and lighter than the Great White, the Mako may reach a maximum length of 13 feet. These sharks have a very pointed nose and a much less prominent dorsal fin than its cousin the Great White. It may be the swiftest shark and is the only shark that can go fast enough to catch up with swordfish and mackerel. It is a very active shark, sometimes even leaping out of the water. Its teeth are rather sharp and slender. Because of its leaping ability and activity, it is the only shark sought as a game fish. Makos have a bad reputation and are considered dangerous. They are handsomely colored, being cobalt blue or ultramarine blue on their dorsal surface and sides, while their belly is snow white.

**Distribution:** Found in tropical and warmer temperate waters of the Atlantic Ocean. A related species is found in the Pacific.

## Tiger Sharks (Carcharinidae): Dangerous Man-Eaters

The largest family of sharks, the Carcharinidae, contains a number of dangerous so-called man-eaters, the most notorious of which is

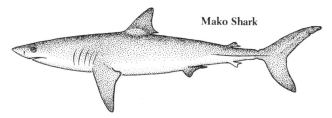

Mako Shark

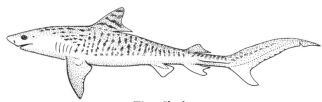

Tiger Shark

the Tiger Shark, *Galeocerdo cuvieri*. Charcharinds are also called Requiem Sharks, a well deserved name based on the first Latin word in the mass said for the dead. Usually these fearsome predators move slowly, but when in pursuit of food are vigorous, powerful, swift swimmers. Their serrated teeth, which can cut right through the bony carapace of a large sea turtle, can produce horrible wounds on humans. There are well documented human attacks by Tiger Sharks. Tiger Sharks have very short, blunt snouts, and their tails have sharp points. They are striped like a tiger (hence the name) when they are younger, but as they grow older, the stripes become less prominent and they appear gray or gray-brown on their dorsal surface and sides and somewhat lighter below. The largest recorded Tiger Shark was 18 feet long, but most are smaller. They are one of the most common large sharks found in tropical waters.

**Distribution:** An oceanic species that often is found in shallow waters in all tropical and subtropical oceans.

## Lake Nicaragua Sharks (*Carcharinus nicaraguensis*): Dangerous

The requiem shark family boasts of the only fresh-water shark, *Carcharinus nicaraguensis*. The Nicaragua Shark, as its name implies, is found only in Lake Nicaragua and the rivers that empty

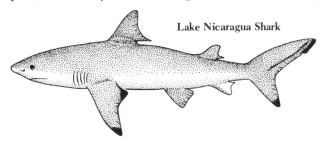

Lake Nicaragua Shark

into it. A rather small shark, usually less than ten feet long, it commonly cruises in rather shallow waters, and a number of human attacks have occurred in the waters of Lake Nicaragua. It is dark gray with a light underbelly. Given the dangerous political situation in Nicaragua today, the odds are that you may never encounter one of these sharks.

## Lemon Sharks (*Negaprion brevirostris*): Possibly Dangerous

Another requiem shark found inshore around docks, saltwater bays, and creeks is the Lemon Shark, *Negaprion brevirostris*. A number of shark attacks in the coastal waters of South Carolina have been attributed to this species. It derives its name from its yellow-brown color and yellow or olive-yellow belly. It has a blunt, rounded snout. Its second dorsal fin is almost as large as the first dorsal, and it seldom is more than ten feet long.

**Distribution:** Shallow Atlantic coastal waters as far north as North Carolina.

## Bull Sharks (*Carcharinus leuces*):Possibly Dangerous

Although not usually considered a man-eater, the shark that you are most likely to run into in shallow waters and even in the entrances to salt-water rivers is the stout-bodied Bull Shark, *Carcharinus leuces*. These sharks are seldom encountered far from the shore, and they have even worked their way up the lower Mississippi River. They are probably related to the Lake Nicaragua Shark and the Ganges River and Zambesi River Sharks, both

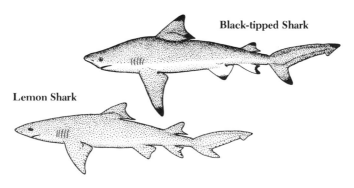

**Black-tipped Shark**

**Lemon Shark**

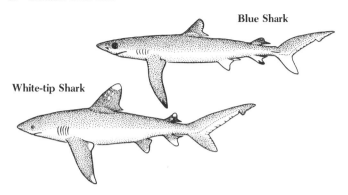

of which have been reported as ferocious attackers of human bathers. On the African coast of Natal, where many attacks occur, the Bull Shark is reputed to be one of the offenders. The Bull Sharks off the coasts of the Americas have no such reputation, but they can reach lengths of up to ten feet and do represent a potential hazard to bathers and snorkelers.

## Blue Sharks (*Prionace glauca*), White-Tip Sharks (*Pterolamiops longimanus*): Dangerous

There have been reports by seamen after a maritime disaster in deep oceanic waters that they were repeatedly attacked by packs of sharks. There are two members of the requiem shark family reliably accused of being man-eaters in such situations: The handsome, long-snouted Blue Shark, *Prionace glauca*, which may reach lengths of twelve feet, and the White-Tip Shark, *Pterolamiops longimanus*, a solitary fearless hunter of 13 feet or more. The Blue Shark has a very distinctive shape and color, while the White-Tip can readily be distinguished by its rounded, white-tipped dorsal fin. Sometimes the caudal, pectoral, and pelvic fins also are white-tipped.

**Distribution:** Both are numerous in the deep tropical waters of the tropical and subtropical Atlantic.

## Crocodiles and Alligators (*Crocodilia*)

The reptile order Crocodilia includes true crocodiles, of the family Crocodylidae, and alligators, of the family Alligatoridae. Both families are amphibious, and are bound to a life on the banks of

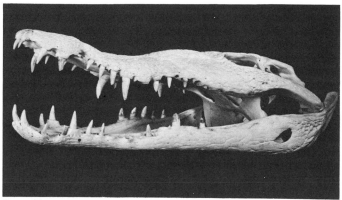

Crocodile

streams, rivers, and lakes, where they swim, hunt, lay eggs, and rear their young. All have pitted armored plates on the back and tail, and they have elongated skulls that have the skin directly attached to the bones. They swim by movements of their powerful tails and while swimming fold their legs back against their bodies. They can walk and run in an ungainly manner, but usually when on land lie on their bellies. Sometimes they are found quite far inland, and despite their awkwardness can move with considerable speed for short distances. Often when sunning themselves they lie with their mouths open, possibly as a means of temperature regulation. (**Plate 11.**)

Crocs and alligators have nostrils placed on top of their snouts, are air breathers, and float in the water with eyes, nostrils, and ears sticking slightly out of the water. They are both hunters and scavengers, and have powerful jaws lined with conical teeth. They will attack and eat large animals which they seize, pull under water, and then rotate to tear off edible-sized chunks. A large victim will often be stuffed under some roots for a later feast.

Crocodiles may be distinguished from alligators by their tooth arrangement. Both have enlarged fourth lower teeth. In crocodiles this tooth sits in a notch on the upper jaw, is clearly visible, and gives the croc the appearance of having a narrowed snout. Alligators, on the other hand, have their enlarged fourth lower teeth fitting into a pit in the upper jaw; hence, these teeth are invisible and the snout appears broader.

Alligators may live 30 or more years, and crocodiles 20 or more years. They grow continually, and the adult American alligator averages about ten feet in length, while the largest recorded reached slightly over 19 feet. The American crocodile is even larger, averaging 12 feet and reaching recorded lengths of 23 feet. While alligators and crocodiles seldom attack humans, there are well documented cases of attacks on people, and human remains have been found in the bowels of dead alligators. The American crocodile is a highly endangered species, but the American alligator is currently enjoying a population explosion and is becoming a pest in some southern states. Alligators are also predators of domestic pets in these areas.

**Distribution:** American crocodiles of various species are found in Cuba, southeastern Mexico, and eastern Guatemala, and in limited numbers on the southern tip of Florida. They are protected and can be found in both fresh and salt water.

The American alligator, *Alligator mississipiensis*, is found in swamps, bayous, rivers, and lakes. Its northern limit is the Carolinas, and it can be seen in Georgia, Florida, Mississippi, Alabama, Louisiana, and Texas, and into Mexico.

**Prevention and Control:** Any crocodile or alligator over eight feet long can kill an adult human. They are not pets, nor are they particularly friendly. They are fine when embroidered on a tennis shirt, but otherwise keep your distance. In gator country be particularly careful with children and pets.

# PART III

# Reptiles That Envenomate

## Gila Monsters (*Heloderma suspectum*) (Rarely ☠ )

Gila (Heéla) Monsters of the southwest United States and western Mexico are the only poisonous lizards among 3000 species of lizard. They belong to the family Helodermatidae, which has been around for thirty-five million years. There are two species, *Heloderma suspectum* and the Mexican beaded lizard, *Heloderma horridum.* Both are heavy-bodied, plump, sluggish animals covered with small bead-like scales which are patterned with pink, yellow, orange, and black mottled blotches. Their tails are blunt, and when the lizards are well fed become plump, since they are fat reservoirs. They are maximally active at night, when they use their long, thick, forked tongues to taste the air and locate prey: eggs, birds, small mammals. They have extremely powerful jaws and can attack with surprising agility.

The poison apparatus consists of venom glands on the outside of the lower jaw that empty into ducts which carry the venom to the flanged and grooved teeth of the lower jaw. Like poisonous snakes, they may not envenomate all the time. The venom contains a pain-producing substance (serotonin), enzymes which

**Gila Monster**

break down tissue, anticlotting agents, and a neurotoxin which has not been completely characterized. Envenomation occurs when the monster has secured a firm hold for several minutes. The bite is bulldog-like, and the mouth often has to be pried open to get free of the beast.

Gila Monsters reach a maximum length of two feet, although the average adult is about a foot and a half long. They mate in July and lay three to fifteen eggs in moist sand, where they hatch in about thirty days.

**Distribution:** *H. suspectum* is found in Arizona and extends south into Mexico. Its northern limit is southwest Utah and nearby California. *H. Horridum* is found in western Mexico. Both species are found in sandy or gravelly soils where there are shrubs and are particularly active during the rainy season and at night. They are often found in burrows or under rocks. (**Plate 12.**)

**Bite and Symptoms:** There have been a number of deaths recorded in which Gila Monsters are at least in part responsible. Most victims were usually drunk, ill, or both when they were bitten. Symptoms depend on several factors, including the size of both the lizard and the victim. The duration of the bite and the number of teeth involved determine the amount of venom injected. Symptoms include pain, swelling, sweating, vomiting, bleeding around the bite, excessive salivation, shallow rapid breathing, muscle weakness, exaggerated reflexes, swelling of the tongue, and in extreme cases, shock and paralysis.

**Prevention:** Gila monsters are shy and bites occur when people try to pick them up.

**First Aid:** Get the monster off by placing it on the ground and pouring anything unpleasant into its mouth—ammonia, alcohol, lighter fluid, gasoline, etc. This may cause it to let go. If flame is available, a campfire or lighter or pack of matches can be applied under the lizard's jaw. It is very difficult to pry the jaws open. Clean wound and get victim to physician.

**Medical Treatment:** Treat symptomatically if there is no antivenin available. Give tetanus shot and be alert for infection.

# SNAKES (SERPENTES): AN INTRODUCTION

There are some 2700 species of snakes throughout the world, with twelve or 13 families found in North America, where they range from the Canadian Northwest southward to Panama. Snakes possess elongated cylindrical bodies without the clear body divisions seen in other vertebrates. They are covered with scaly skins, lack limbs, have no external auditory openings, and stare at you with unblinking, lidless eyes. Their lifestyles vary; some are subterranean, some terrestrial, some are tree climbers, and some are water dwellers. Some snakes are active by day, and others are mainly nocturnal hunters. All snakes are carnivores, meat eaters, and they can be found from sea level to over ten thousand feet up in the mountains.

Snakes grow throughout their life spans and episodically shed their old outer skins in one piece. Snakes may either lay eggs or bear live young. They hunt by vision, by vibration, by smell, and some by means of specialized heat sensors. They can unhinge their jaws and swallow their prey whole. Because they have no breastbones, and elastic skins they can swallow prey whose girth is greater than theirs. Some snakes, particularly those in warmer climates, are active all year long, while those snakes found in colder climates hibernate through the winter, as do other cold-blooded creatures.

One of the most disturbing characteristics about snakes is their retractible, darting, forked tongue. Contrary to myth that the tongue is a venom delivery apparatus, the tongue is primarily used as a part of the snake's olfactory apparatus, and indeed many snakes have a remarkably keen sense of smell.

## Snake Movement

Serpentine movement is accomplished by lateral undulations of the body. These coordinated muscular movements produce thrust of the curves of its body against the ground. The longer the snake the more curves, and the greater the number of points of thrust against the ground. This crawling type of locomotion over flat ground is not very effective, and most snakes move rather slowly, only four to five miles per hour. They can also move by concertina-type movements over difficult ground and in narrow burrows. Snakes can move rapidly through dense networks of branches, and they have mastered the art of climbing. They are also excellent swimmers. Swimming snakes, such as the Water Moccasin, are incapable of striking while in the water. A few snakes, such as some Central America *Bothrops*, have learned to jump when striking at a prey.

One type of movement, however, is lightning fast, and that is the strike at an intruder or prey. To achieve this, the snake usually coils and forms one or more "S" shaped curves. In straightening these curves, the head shoots forward for about a third of the snake's length.

## Venomous Snakes

There are about sixty species of venomous snakes in North and Central America. The majority of these species belong to the family Viperidae, and all of these vipers are equipped with heat-sensng facial pits, hence are called pit vipers. The second family of poisonous snakes, cousins to the deadly cobras, are the Elapidae, which are represented by several species of coral snakes. Somewhat related to the Elapidae is the third family, the Hydrophidae, of which only one representative, the Yellow-Bellied Sea Snake of the Pacific Gulf of Panama, is found in our hemisphere. The elapids and hyrdophids have medium-length fixed fangs and are in general far more placid than the viperid snakes.

## The Pit Vipers (Viperidae)

Pit vipers are found all over the world, and almost three hundred species of snakes are found in this family. There are five genera of these venomous snakes inhabiting North and Central America. These are: the *Agkistrodon*, represented by the Cottonmouth Moccasins and Copperheads; Rattlesnakes, represented by the genera *Crotalus* and *Sistrurus;* the Bushmaster (one genus, *Lachesis*); and the American Lanceheads, *Bothrops*. The first three genera are characterized by a distinct neck and wide, triangular-shaped heads. *Lachesis*, the Bushmaster, is a large, slender snake, and the Lanceheads, as their name implies, have pointed heads reminiscent of a spearhead.

Pit vipers have evolved a pair of remarkable heat-sensing organs located below and behind the nostrils and in front of the eyes.

Pit Viper

These pits are capable of locating a warm-bodied prey even in total darkness, and allow the snake to strike with remakable accuracy within five degrees of dead center. At 50 cm these infrared or heat sensors can detect temperature differences of less than half a degree Celsius. Differences in temperature between the two pits permit the snake to determine direction and distance. The field of each heat-sensing pit extends to either side of the body and above and below the horizontal plane by about 50 degrees. In real life the snakes integrate signals from both the heat sensors and visual information from the eyes to locate their prey. The viperid eyes are striking because they are lidless and the pupils are vertical elliptical slits.

Many pit vipers, including the Bushmaster and the Moccasin, vibrate their tails as a warning to stay away. This behavior is particularly evident in the most highly evolved pit vipers, the rattlesnakes. The rattlesnakes bear on their tails a unique structure composed of a series of interlocking, flexible, dry segments made of horny modified scales. This rattle when vibrated vigorously produces a buzzing sound. When the snake is agitated, or prior to its striking, this rattle is vibrated, although some snakes, like the Mexican rattler, the Cascabel, will sound only a single click or two before striking, and sometimes rattlers will strike without any warning buzz. However, many rattlers simply announce their presence with the sound, and it is a warning to stay away. The rattle starts out as a terminal button, and a new segment of the rattle is added each time the snake sheds its skin. Shedding occurs two to four times a year; thus, a twenty-year-old rattle could theoretically have as many as 80 segments in its rattle. In nature segments are often lost, and more usually the rattle of a mature snake may have only a dozen segments.

**The Venom Apparatus:** Venom glands are modified salivary glands that are capable of secreting venom. The development of these glands is greatest in the pit vipers. The glands are located on each side of the head behind and below the eyes. Each gland is a flattened sac-like structure which is surrounded by voluntary muscle. The snake can control the amount of contraction and thus control the quantity of venom ejected. Leading from the poison gland is a long, thin canal or duct. This duct swings up under the eye past the back of the heat-sensing pit organ and then travels to the front of the fang sheath. The venom then travels through an opening in the top front of the fang, down the hollow fang, and is ejected through a slit-like opening at the front of the fang. There is some controversy regarding how much venom is ejected with

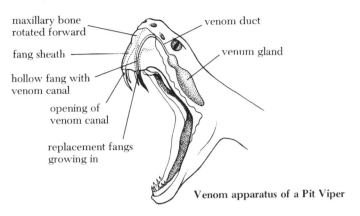

maxillary bone rotated forward

venom duct

fang sheath

venom gland

hollow fang with venom canal

opening of venom canal

replacement fangs growing in

**Venom apparatus of a Pit Viper**

malicious intent. Possibly only 8 percent of the available venom is discharged in a single bite. Thus, there is plenty left, and subsequent strikes can still deliver a potentially lethal dose. The snake continuously manufactures new venom to replace its depleted supply, and it may take a week or more to fill the gland. (See illustration above.)

**Snake Venom:** Snake venom is a complex mix of many components, mainly proteins, including some very potent enzymes. It was once thought that the enzymes were the main villains in producing toxic effects. While it is true that these enzymes are capable of causing much damage, such as disrupting cell membranes and breaking down the cement that holds cells together, the most important toxic effects are probably caused by smaller peptide components of the venom. These poisonous components produce cellular mayhem in several ways. First, they may inactivate some basic body defense mechanisms such as the clotting system and the complement system. Secondly, they may trigger or activate a number of the body's own inflammatory substances such as histamine, kinins, prostaglandins, and other biologically potent substances, and finally, they can have direct effects on the nervous system.

We used to break snake venoms down into three main groups: Neurotoxins, which act directly on nerve cells or synapses between nerves and muscles, Hemotoxins, which act on blood cells, and Cytotoxins, which act directly on cells. According to Dr. Findlay Russell, such a classification is misleading and can lead to mistakes in diagnosing clinical symptoms, since each type of toxin can have a variety of effects. Thus, in crotalid bites there are usually a number of simultaneous toxic responses. Nevertheless, the old concepts have some value in looking at the venoms of different pit vipers, because some contain a preponderance of toxins that act mainly on the blood, and others have a relatively high concentration of neurotoxins.

**Toxicity of Venoms:** The relative toxicity of venoms is difficult to establish precisely. The usual procedure is to determine how much it takes to kill an experimental animal. Toxicity is always a function of the amount of venom per unit body weight and measures the dose needed to kill 50 percent of the animals injected. Even using this technique, there is still some controversy. Clearly the most toxic venom is that of the sea snakes. The Yellow-Bellied Sea Snake found in the Pacific off Panama has a venom so potent that .09 millionths of a gram per gram of mouse is fatal 50 percent of the time. Among the pit vipers, the Central American rattlesnake, the Cascabel, has the most deadly toxin, .35 millionths of a gram per gram of mouse. The next most deadly is the fer-de-lance, *Bothrops*, at .46 millionths of a gram per gram of mouse. The rattlesnakes found in the United States, such as the infamous Eastern Diamondback, has a much less toxic venom, 2.4 millionths of a gram per gram of mouse, and the much feared Bushmaster is less than half this potent. The severity of a pit viper bite is influenced by several factors, the most important of which is the amount of venom injected. Angry or wounded snakes inject larger amounts of venom. Larger snakes inject relatively larger amounts of venom. Although the figures gleaned from the literature reflect general levels of toxicity, there is a great deal of variability—age, season of year, interval between feeding, and subspecies all contribute to the variability. The response in humans is also dependent on the age, weight, location of bite, and health of the bite victim. Copperhead has the least toxic venom of any of the common pit vipers, ten millionths of a gram per gram of mouse. It is obvious from the foregoing data that: (1) smaller snake bite victims, such as children, are at greater risk because of their slight weight, and (2) different species vary widely in poison content.

It should be pointed out that relative toxicity of snake venom is related to the age of the snake, and thus the venom of young rattlesnakes may be fifteen times more potent than the venom of an adult. One report suggested that the pit viper venom reaches its maximum toxicity at eight months, and then declines after that. It should also be apparent that the amount of venom injected is important, since the snakes with some of the worst reputations have relatively less toxic venom. This is because large snakes like the Bushmaster, Eastern Diamondback, and Western Dia-

**YIELD AND LETHALITY OF VENOMS OF IMPORTANT POISONOUS SNAKES**

| Snake | Average length of adult (inches) | Approximate yield, dry venom (mg) | Intraperitoneal $Ld_{50}$ (mg/kg) |
|---|---|---|---|
| North America | | | |
| A. Rattlesnakes (*Crotalus*) | | | |
| Eastern diamondback (*C. adamanteus*) | 33–65 | 370–720 | 1.89 |
| Western diamondback (*C. atrox*) | 30–65 | 175–325 | 3.71 |
| Timber (*C. horridus horridus*) | 32–54 | 95–150 | 2.91 |
| Prairie (*C. viridis viridis*) | 32–46 | 25–100 | 2.25 |
| Southern Pacific (*C. v. helleri*) | 30–48 | 75–160 | 1.60 |
| Red diamond (*C. ruber ruber*) | 30–52 | 125–400 | 6.69 |
| Mojave (*C. scutulatus*) | 22–40 | 50–90 | 0.23 |
| Sidewinder (*C. cerastes*) | 18–30 | 18–40 | 4.00 |
| B. Moccasins (*Agkistrodon*) | | | |
| Cottonmouth (*A. piscivorus*) | 30–50 | 90–148 | 5.11 |
| Copperhead (*A. contortrix*) | 24–36 | 40–72 | 10.50 |
| C. Coral snakes (*Micrurus*) | | | |
| Eastern coral snake (*M. fulvius*) | 16–28 | 2–6 | 0.97 |
| Central America | | | |
| A. Rattlesnakes (*Crotalus*) | | | |
| Cascabel (*C. durissus*) | 20–48 | 20–40 | 0.30 |
| B. American lance-headed vipers (*Bothrops*) | | | |
| Barba amarilla (*B. atrox*) | 46–80 | 70–160 | 3.80 |
| C. Bushmaster (*Lachesis mutus*) | 70–110 | 280–450 | 5.93 |

Table from *Poisonous Snakes of the World* NAV. MED. P 5099

57

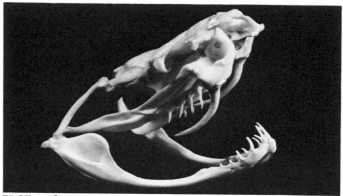

**Pit Viper, fangs erect**

mondback inject very large amounts of venom. In Table One the venom yield for a number of poisonous American snakes is summarized, along with the relative toxicity of the venom.

**Teeth and Fangs:** Snakes' teeth are pointed, curve backwards, and are fused to the jawbones. At regular intervals, old teeth, including fangs, are shed and replaced by new ones. Fangs are enlarged teeth fused to the maxillary bones, usually in the front of the upper jaw. However, there are some back-fanged snakes. In venomous snakes, particularly the pit vipers, the fangs are extremely long. When the viper's mouth is closed, the fangs are folded back against the upper jaw. Even when the mouth is open, the fangs remain retracted, but as the viper strikes, muscular action rotates the mobile maxillary bones and brings the fangs into an erect position. Thus, the fangs don't move, but the bones to which they are fused do (see photos on facing page). When the

**Bushmaster, fangs retracted**

snake strikes, its jaws are opened so wide (180°) that the pointed tips of the fangs point forward, and fangs enter as a jab or rapier thrust. Then the jaws close to imbed the fangs deeper. Even with this rapid thrust-bite, most wounds are relatively superficial. The actual strike is so fast it is hard to follow. In reality the head moves forward before the mouth opens, and the fangs are erected only at the last moment. The fangs themselves are hollow, with an elongated opening at their tips.

Actually, most pit vipers have a characteristic warning behavior that includes tail vibration and form a coil with the head held back with one or more "S"-shaped loops, ready to strike. The tail is forward, upright, and often vibrating, and the tongue is held out without its usual flicking movement. If you see a snake in this position, back off; the snake is sending a very clear message, "don't tread on me."

## Snake Bites (15 to 25 Fatalities per Year in the United States)

According to Dr. F. Russell, upwards of 45,000 humans in the United States are bitten by snakes every year. The vast majority of these bites are by harmless, non-venomous snakes that have been disturbed by humans. People in general and children in particular have a predilection for trying to catch snakes. A harmless snake has rows of sharp teeth in both the upper and lower jaw which produce a pattern of pinprick-sized holes. Often we reflexively draw away upon being bitten, and this sometimes produces multiple scratches. Such snakebites, while mildly painful, are no cause for alarm but should be cleaned with an antiseptic (or soap and water) as soon as possible, because any time the skin is broken there is a possibility of infection.

There are about seven thousand venomous snake bites in the United States in an average year. Most of these bites, about 60 percent, are caused by Rattlesnakes, the remainder by other pit vipers (Copperheads, Water Moccasins) and Coral Snakes, although the shy and retiring Coral Snake is responsible for very few bites, only one percent. Thus, the main culprits are pit vipers. The bite pattern from these pit vipers is distinctive, usually showing two deep larger puncture wounds and then sometimes smaller pinpricks. Actually most pit vipers bite and instantly let go. Their prey is usually small mammals, and once they have bitten they track their dying prey with their keen sense of smell. Sixty-five percent of all pit viper bites leave two distinct fang marks. Twenty-four percent only show one fang mark, and eleven percent show three or more fang marks—the latter case because

**Table 2**

### SYMPTOMS AND SIGNS OF BITES

| Symptoms and Signs[1] | North American Rattlesnakes (Crotalus) | Central and South American Rattlesnakes (Crotalus) | North American Moccasins (Agkistrodon) | American Lance-headed Vipers (Bothrops) |
|---|---|---|---|---|
| Swelling and edema | + + +[5] | + | + + | + + + |
| Pain | + + | + + | + | + + + |
| Discoloration of skin | + + + | + | + | + + + |
| Blisters | + + + |  | + | + + + |
| Bruise-like bleeding under skin | + + + | + | + + | + + + |
| Superficial blood vessels clot | + + |  | − | + + |
| Death of tissue around bite | + + |  | + | + + + |
| Loss of tissue | + + |  | − | + + + |
| Weakness | + + | + + + | + | + + + |
| Thirst | + + | + + | + | + + |
| Nausea or vomiting or both | + + | + + | + | + + |
| Diarrhea | + | + + | − | + |
| Weak pulse and changes in rate | + + + | + + + | + | + + + |
| Hypotension or shock | + + + | + | + | + + + |
| Destruction of red blood cells | + + + | − | − | + + + |
| Increased clotting time | + + + | + | − | + + + |
| Bleeding[2] | + + + | − | + | + + + |
| Anemia, loss of red cells | + + | − | − | + + |

| | | | | |
|---|---|---|---|---|
| Blood platelet changes[3] | + + | − | − | + + |
| Sugar in urine | + + | − | + | + + |
| Protein in urine | + + | + | + | + + |
| Tingling or numbness[4] | + + | + + + | + | + + |
| Twitching | + | + + | − | + |
| Muscular weakness or paralysis | + | + + + | − | + |
| Drooping eyelid | + | + + + | − | + |
| Blurring of vision | + | + + + | − | + |
| Respiratory distress | + + | + | + | + + |
| Swelling regional lymph nodes | + + | + + | + | + + |
| Abnormal electrocardiogram | + | + | − | + |
| Coma | + | + + | − | + |

[1]In the more severe cases the intensity of the symptoms and signs may be markedly increased. In addition, there may be severe respiratory distress, purple lips, nails, cyanosis, muscle spasms and secondary shock leading to death.

[2]Bleeding may be from the gastrointestinal, urinary, or respiratory tracts, from the gums, or it may be subcutaneous. Bleeding from the gums is common following *Bothrops* envenomation.

[3]Platelets may be increased in mild poisoning and markedly decreased in severe cases.

[4]Often confined to the tongue and mouth, but may involve the scalp and distal parts of the toes and fingers as well as the injured part.

[5](+ to + + +) = Grading of severity of symptom, sign, or finding, (−) = Of lesser significance or absent, ( ) = Information lacking.

Table from *Poisonous Snakes of the World* NAV. MED. P 5099

**Eastern Diamondback Rattlesnake striking**
*Photo courtesy of Thomaston Mills, North Carolina*

often the pit vipers bring replacement fangs into line before shedding their old fangs.

Most venomous snake bites on humans occur on the hand, arm, ankle, or lower leg. The majority of pit vipers usually strike only out of a coiled position and can reach out only about one-third their length. Their strike is slightly upward but mostly straight ahead. Thus, wearing a good pair of leather high-topped boots or rattler chaps (see photo above) will protect your lower leg from most medium-sized pit vipers. However, large rattlers like the Eastern and Western Diamondbacks can strike as high as mid-thigh.

Males are much more frequently bitten than females. Most victims of bites by venomous snakes, about 60 percent, are under 20 years of age. Children in particular are vulnerable, and 35 percent of all poisonous snake bites occur in children under the age of ten.

Venomous snakes can voluntarily control the amount of venom they inject and sometimes they do not envenomate at all. It is estimated that 20 percent of all rattlesnake bites do not involve injection of venom. Copperheads and Cottonmouth Moccasins don't envenomate 30 percent of the time. Coral snakes envenomate only 50 percent of the time, and the very poisonous sea snakes envenomate only 40 percent of the time. Furthermore, rattlesnakes can control the amount of venom they inject, and while there is some controversy about how much venom is injected in a single strike, there are reports that the second and even the third strike can deliver a potentially lethal dose. Since the amount of venom injected is under the voluntary control of the snake, it makes good sense not to provoke or annoy a snake.

About 15 to 25 people per year die of snake bite in the United States. Most bites occur in snake belts found in the South and Southwest, the Rockies, the West Coast, and Eastern mountains. Only three states are free of venomous snakes, Hawaii, Maine, and Alaska. However, lethality figures do not tell the whole story about the hazard of snake bite, since sometimes the victim will experience considerable tissue loss, scar tissue formation and residual nerve damage, including blindness. A few severe cases—about eleven percent—of envenomations that are not treated quickly enough can require amputation.

Not only people are bitten by venomous snakes but pets, particularly dogs, are frequently bitten, and the usual culprit, 80 percent of the time, is a rattlesnake. Dogs, in general, are curious creatures, often sniffing anything that moves. This behavior makes dogs particularly vulnerable to being bitten about the face and shoulders. The pit viper's strike is so fast that the dog has little chance to back off. It is estimated that twenty thousand domesticated animals and pets are bitten each year, and smaller animals are frequently killed because they receive a relatively larger amount of venom per unit of body weight. Naive dogs, inexperienced with snakes, should not be taken on camping trips where there are poisonous snakes. If you do bring a pet, keep it leashed.

## Guide to First Aid For Venomous Snake Bites

1. Kill offending snake. Warning: do not put hand near dead snake's mouth; bite reflexes may remain. Strike snake behind head with a long, stout stick. Identification of dead snake is important in determining treatment. Usually rattlesnakes can strike from a coil for only one-third their length with considerable accuracy. However, they have been reported to strike a target at half their length if agitated. Thus, a very large rattler can hit you at ranges up to three and a half feet. Even though the snake has already discharged some of its venom, it can still deliver at least one more full load on a second victim. In your enthusiasm to dispatch the offending snake, make sure that you don't get too close.
2. Immobilize injured part in a comfortable position, but at heart level.
3. Reassure victim, calm him. Bites treated quickly are hardly ever lethal. Indeed, 20 percent or more of venomous snake bites do not involve the injection of poison.

## Usual symptoms of Pit Viper envenomation

Note: These symptoms may vary with different species of pit vipers. See Table showing symptoms and signs

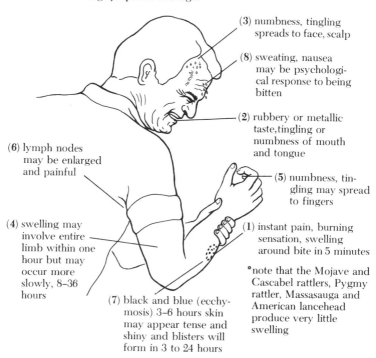

(3) numbness, tingling spreads to face, scalp

(8) sweating, nausea may be psychological response to being bitten

(2) rubbery or metallic taste, tingling or numbness of mouth and tongue

(6) lymph nodes may be enlarged and painful

(5) numbness, tingling may spread to fingers

(4) swelling may involve entire limb within one hour but may occur more slowly, 8–36 hours

(1) instant pain, burning sensation, swelling around bite in 5 minutes

°note that the Mojave and Cascabel rattlers, Pygmy rattler, Massasauga and American lancehead produce very little swelling

(7) black and blue (ecchymosis) 3–6 hours skin may appear tense and shiny and blisters will form in 3 to 24 hours

*later symptoms of envenomation*
Drooping eyelids, blurred vision, chills, fever, drop in blood pressure, shock, hemorrhage, discoloration of bitten appendage, tissue destruction, thirst, muscle weakness, paralysis and respiratory distress

4. Wipe off the wound to remove any venom on the skin surface.
5. Apply a wide constriction band (not a tourniquet) within the first few minutes. It is not much use after 15 minutes. Constriction band is applied between the wound and the heart two to three inches above wound. It should be only tight enough to cut off flow in surface or superficial veins and lymph vessels, and should not block arterial blood flow. (You should still be able to feel a pulse below the constriction.)
6. ONLY IF MEDICAL TREATMENT IS MORE THAN AN HOUR AWAY AND SWELLING OCCURS FIVE TO 15 MINUTES AFTER BITE, make an incision ¼ inch long and ⅛

inch deep directly through each fang mark with a sharp blade. Do not overdo the cutting. _____ This is ¼ of an inch. __ This is ⅛ of an inch.

7. Apply suction to incision: mouth suction is okay unless you have gum problems or a break in the mouth mucosa. However, it is preferable to use commercially available suction devices. Institute suction quickly, since suction applied 15 to 20 minutes after the bite does not do much good. Keep suction up until you get the victim to the doctor. Suction is useless in Coral Snake bites.

8. Get patient to physician as quickly as possible—bring dead snake if possible.

## First Aid Do Nots

1. No ice packs.
2. Do not use incision-suction unless you are more than an hour from medical treatment.
3. Do not use tight tourniquet.
4. Do not use alcohol on wound or in mouth of victim.
5. Do not give any medication.

**Medical Treatment:** While there is some controversy regarding the preferred treatment, in this book the author has chosen to follow the guidelines set by Dr. Findlay Russell. He is one of the most outstanding authorities on animal venoms and clinical treatment of envenomation, and has treated over 1000 cases of snake bite.

First, what *not* to do: (1) Do not use cryotherapy. It does not slow down or inactivate the enzymes in the snakes. Indeed, according to Dr. Russell, cooling may even force the enzymes into deeper tissues where blood vessels are undamaged. (2) Do not initially use large doses of antiflammatory steroids. According to Dr. Russell, steroids during the first six to eight hours may increase the action of the venom or somehow block the action of the crotalid antivenin. (3) Do not perform fasciotomy to relieve the edema. The edema does not impair the circulation, as Russell and others have shown using the Doppler technique. Hence, the bite victim can be treated without fasciotomy. (4) Establish your diagnosis before starting antivenin. According to Dr. Russell, the symptoms of envenomation occur producing a basically consistent picture (see section on symptoms).

If there are no symptoms after half an hour or more after the bite and there is no swelling, don't use antivenin, but keep observing victim for a few hours. In any case, do routine lab test (blood typing, cross match, bleeding, clotting, clot retract in time,

### Early treatment of Pit Viper envenomation

start antivenin — mild envenomation, 3 vials; moderate, 5–8 vials; severe, start with 8, be ready to give much more

children start with 5 vials — usually give twice the adult dose

2nd I.V. available in case of allergic reaction to Antivenin

aspirin, morphine, codeine for pain, also mild sedative

be prepared to monitor all vital signs and watch for hypotension

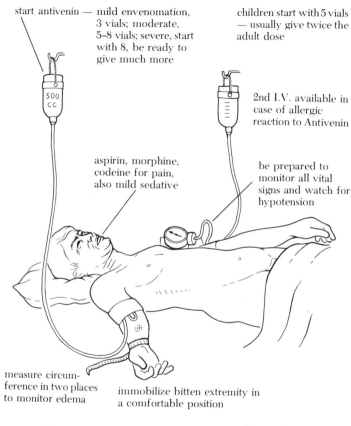

measure circumference in two places to monitor edema

immobilize bitten extremity in a comfortable position

have emergency equipment to treat shock, respiratory problems

laboratory tests (blood typing, cross match, bleeding, clotting, clot retraction time, platelet count, hematocrit CBC, urinalysis, sedimentation rate, prothrombin time)

platelet count, hematocrit CBC, urinalysis) and if severe symptoms develop, also do sedimentation rate and prothrombin time.

Start antivenin. Three vials I.V. in 500 cc drip. If limb is swollen, five to eight vials. If symptoms show severe envenomation, start with eight vials and be prepared to give much more. Keep small amount of Antivenin I.V. for up to twelve hours. Note that children require larger doses. Start them with five vials, and if symptoms appear severe, give twice the adult dose. Ever 15 minutes, measure circumference of bitten extremity at two or more points proximal to bite. If edema continues to increase, give more antivenin. Decrease dose only as symptoms lessen. Be ready to treat for shock, circulatory collapse, tracheotomy. If hemolysis or decrease in blood volume occurs or platelet deficiency develops, give fresh whole blood. Tetanus shot is mandatory. Hold antibiotics until necessary. Give aspirin, codeine, or morphine for pain as needed. Give a mild sedative unless there are respiratory problems. Clean and cover wound, immobilize the envenomated limb in a comfortable position. If debridement is needed, wait until the third day. After three days, evaluate bitten limb for: joint motion, strength, sensation, and girth. Soak bitten part three times a day for 15 minutes in 1:20 Alum Acetate solution. Clean wound daily, paint with triple aqueous dye solution (1:40 gentian violet, 1:400 brilliant green, and 1:1000 acriflavine). Apply polymyxin-bacitracin-neomycin ointment at bed time.

**Reactions to Antivenin:** Crotalid Polyvalent Antivenin (Wyeth Pharmaceutical) is prepared in horse serum, and 70 percent of bite victims show some delayed serum reaction. Because of its allergenic nature, be prepared to counteract antivenin effects. Have another I.V. in place with 5 percent albumin and epinephrine solution and be prepared to deal with anaphylactic shock. When treating with antivenin, be alert for wheal formation or other allergic responses, and if they develop, stop antivenin and give antihistamine such as diphenhydramine, and then continue antivenin. Most patients will exhibit delayed skin reactions, which will require steroid treatment.

## Eastern Diamondback Rattlesnakes (*Crotalus adamanteus*): Most Dangerous ( ☠ )

The most dangerous rattlesnake in the United States is the large, aggressive Eastern Diamondback Rattlesnake, *Crotalus adamanteus*. This boldly patterned handsome snake has a large triangular head and is heavy-bodied, up to four and a half inches in diameter.

**Eastern Diamondback Rattlesnake**

It may weigh up to 15 pounds and has reached a record length of eight feet, although the average adult is only four or five feet long. As its name implies, its back has a bold, dark diamond pattern with light creamy-yellow borders. There are also distinct light diagonal lines on the sides of the head. Like all rattlers, the Diamondback gives birth to live young, usually in July through October. These 12- to 14-inch new-borns have well-developed fangs and venom glands, and while they don't have the capacity to deliver large amounts of venom, their venom may be 15 times more potent than that of adults. (**Plate 3.**)

It is ranked as the number one cause of serious snake bites in the United States because of its enormous fangs and large venom glands, even though its poison is not particularly toxic. It is easily agitated and will hold its ground against an intruder. Its strike is powerful and accurate. It often gives fair warning by rattling vigorously even when you are 20 feet away.

**Distribution and Habitat:** Found exclusively in the southeastern United States, eastern Louisiana, southern Mississippi, Alabama, eastern North and South Carolina, and Florida. It can be found anywhere in its range in pine woods, sand hills, and abandoned farmlands. It is not found in wet or marshy areas, nor is it found above 500 feet.

**Symptoms, Prevention, First Aid, Medical Treatment:** see pages 59 to 65.

## Western Diamondback Rattlesnakes (*Crotalus atrox*): Very Dangerous ( ☠ )

The Western Diamondback Rattlesnake, *Crotalus atrox*, is ranked as the second most important venomous snake in the United States. It is, like its eastern cousin, a stout-bodied snake with a

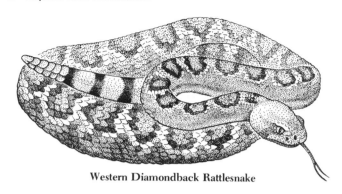

**Western Diamondback Rattlesnake**

large head and distinct neck, but it is not as large. The longest Western Diamondback is just a bit shy of seven feet. Its color pattern of creamy-colored dark diamonds is not as clear as the eastern version, and instead of distinct diamonds there are eight-sided blotches made indistinct by many blackish spots. Because its tail is circled by alternating black and white rings, it is sometimes called the Coontail Rattler. Live young are born in the late summer.

Because this snake ranges over a wide area and is sometimes quite numerous, it causes more serious cases of snake bite than all the other rattlers put together. Although it has shorter fangs and smaller poison glands than the Eastern Diamondback, its venom is more potent. It has been described as nervous, easily aroused, and the most temperamental and aggressive rattlesnake. It angers easily, has a hair-trigger readiness to strike, particularly if it has been injured, and will vigorously defend itself rather than slither away.

A smaller relative of the Western Diamondback, the Red Rattlesnake, *Crotalus ruber*, has red or pink ill-defined diamonds and the same black-and-white coontail. This snake reaches a maximum size of five feet five inches and is found in the very southwest part of California and down the Baja Peninsula. It is much less temperamental and more timid than the Western Diamondback, and its venom is less potent. Nonetheless, it is still a dangerous rattlesnake.

**Distribution and Habitat:** Ranges from southeast Arkansas, throughout most of Texas westward to southeastern California, and southward well into Mexico. It prefers dry, brushy desert areas, rocky bluffs, and canyons, and is found from sea level up to seven thousand feet.

## Mojave Rattlesnakes (*Crotalus scutulatus*): Extremely Dangerous ( ☠ )

The Mojave Rattlesnake, *Crotalus scutulatus,* used to be responsible for more snake bite lethalities in California than all other rattlers. It averages only about three feet in length and the largest reported was only four feet long. It is greenish brown, has a pattern of hexagonal or diamond-shaped blotches bordered by a creamy yellow outline. Like the Western Diamondback, it has a coontail of alternating rings of black and gray. As a matter of fact, it is often confused with the Western Diamondback. (**Plate 10.**)

But this difference is extremely important, because the Mojave rattler bite, for some unknown reason, doesn't cause much local swelling or swelling of the bitten extremity. Consequently, the attending physician may assume there has been little or no envenomation and give too little antivenin. The result may be respiratory paralysis and death twelve to 16 hours later. Dr. Findlay Russell prefers to give twice the amount of antivenin as for other rattlers for Mojave rattler bites. Even the toxicity and nature of the toxin of the Mojave rattler is a matter of controversy. One expert ranks its venom among the most toxic, another among the least toxic of the rattlesnakes. One maintains that it contains a high neurotoxin content, and the other disagrees. It is not a particularly aggressive snake, and doesn't inject much venom, but because of the aforementioned peculiarity of its venom, must be considered extremely dangerous.

**Symptoms, First Aid, Medical Treatment:** See pages 59 to 65.

**Mojave Rattlesnake**

**Habitat and Distribution:** Found in southeast Arizona, southwest California, southern Nevada, and down into Mexico. Usually found in high desert areas and mountain slopes up to eight thousand feet and at sea level at the mouth of the Colorado River. Prefers brush and areas of scrubby growth.

## Timber Rattlesnakes (*Crotalus horridus horridus*), Canebrake Rattlesnakes (*Crotalus horridus articaudatus*): Dangerous

The Timber Rattlesnake, *Crotalus horridus horridus*, and its southern version, the Canebrake Rattlesnake, *Crotalus horridus articaudatus*, are medium-sized rattlers found from Vermont to Florida and as far west as Minnesota and Texas. They are stout-bodied, and the largest recorded *C. horridus* was about six feet two inches long. The Northern or Timber Rattler is yellow, brown, or dark gray with dark blotches. Toward the rear of the snake there are dark cross bands, and the tail is black. The Southerner or Canebrake Rattler is lighter in color, has V-shaped crossbands divided by a reddish-brown stripe running down the back. It too has a black tail. The northern forms are active during the day when the weather is cool, and at night when the weather is warm. (**Plate 5.**)

The Timber rattler and Canebrake rattler are shy, retiring snakes that prefer to retreat rather than stand their ground. Although they rattle noisily when approached, they usually seek cover. However, if backed into a corner, these snakes will defend themselves with vigor.

The northern form can withstand relatively cold temperatures

**Timber Rattlesnake**

and finds a den below the frost line to winter over. These hibernating dens are shared not only with many other rattlesnakes but also with Copperheads and non-venomous Rat snakes.

**Habitat and Distribution:** *C. horridus horridus* is found from northern Vermont southward to northern Georgia and Alabama and can be found as far west as north central Texas, while *C. h. articaudatus* ranges from southern Virginia down through Florida and the southern states to southeast Texas. The northern form prefers remote rocky hillsides and rocky outcroppings up to six thousand feet. The southern forms like moist flood plains and swampy thickets from sea level up. See section on pit vipers for prevention, symptoms, first aid, and medical treatment.

## Western Rattlesnakes (*Crotalus viridis*): Dangerous

There are a number of western Rattlesnakes that are subspecies of *Crotalus viridis*. Their common names are: the Southern Pacific Rattlesnake, which is responsible for the most bites in California, the Hopi Rattler, the Prairie Rattler, the Grand Canyon Rattler, and several others. There is considerable difference in size and color. Most have brown blotches on their backs, often outlined in a lighter color. They may be the western version of the Timber Rattler. These snakes often are irritable and aggressive in their

**Western Rattlesnake**

behavior. They may be numerous, and like many crotalids, may get together in large numbers in a common den to hibernate through the winter.

Their venom is not particularly toxic, and their strike lacks the punch of a Diamondback; hence, envenomation is often superficial. Sometimes these snakes simply spew their venom as they withdraw from a bite. Therefore, it is always a good idea to wipe this off before any of it gets absorbed. These snakes, while not particularly deadly, are dangerous.

**Habitat and Distribution:** From southwest Canada southward to Mexico found from sea level up to the timberline in the Rockies.

## Sidewinders (*Crotalus cerastes*): Mildly Dangerous

The Sidewinder Rattlesnake, *Crotalus cerastes*, is a small (17 to 33 inches long), thick-bodied snake noted for its peculiar sidewinding means of locomotion. It is easily identified by two triangular horn-like projections formed on the scales above each eye. Sidewinders are mainly active at night, and during the day they seek shelter in animal burrows or under bushes. As they move through the sand they leave a distinctive track of parallel J-shaped marks.

This snake has un undeserved lethal reputation, perhaps because of its peculiar horns, or locomotion, or possibly because the Air Force has named its deadly heat-seeking air-to-air missile the Sidewinder. The Sidewinder does not have a particularly aggressive disposition, and its toxin is not among the most toxic, but it can deliver a nasty bite if provoked and, like all rattlesnakes, should only be viewed from a safe distance. (**Plate 6.**)

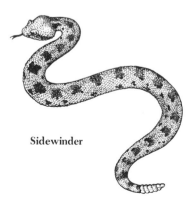

Sidewinder

**Habitat and Distribution:** The roughly scaled Sidewinders, of which there are three subspecies, are found in eastern California, southern Nevada, southern Utah, in the Mojave, Sonora, and Arizona, ranging down the Baja Peninsula and into western Mexico.

**Symptoms, First Aid and Medical Treatment:** See pages 59 to 65.

## Massasauga Rattlesnakes (*Sistrurus catenatus*), Pygmy Rattlesnakes (*Sistrurus miliarius*): Mildly Dangerous

Closely related to the Copperheads and Cottonmouths is a genus of small rattlesnakes, *Sistrurus*, of which there are only two North American representatives, the tiny Pygmy Rattlesnake, *Sistrurus miliarius*, and the Massasauga, *S. catenatus*. Like the genus *Agkistrodon*, they have enlarged scales (nine of them) forming a symmetrical shield on top of their heads. The Massasauga reaches a maximum length of three feet, and is brownish or grayish with a row of brown blotches on its back and on either side. It has a stubby tail, tipped with a small but well-developed rattle. They are mainly frog eaters, but will take a mouse or bird if it is available. They are often found in moist areas, and some people refer to them as swamp rattlers; in Chippewa the name translates to "great river mouth." (**Plate 9.**)

Pygmy Rattlesnake

Massasauga Rattlesnake

The Massasauga has typical pit viper fangs and venom apparatus, although in a dwarf version. Its venom is more toxic than that of Copperheads and Moccasins, but the bite, while seldom lethal, can be serious, and the Massasauga is responsible for a considerable number of bites.

The Pygmy Rattler or Ground Rattlesnake is tiny, usually only 16 to 20 inches long, although a 30-inch specimen has been recorded. It has a tiny rattle at the end of its tiny tail, and you can hardly hear it rattle beyond six feet, and even then it sounds like a buzzing insect. The Pygmy Rattler is dark gray and has a line of irregular, dark, somewhat rounded blotches on its back. On the neck and middle of the back, the spaces between the blotches are red. The tail is also red, while the underside is white with black spots. It will strike when angered with a series of vicious jabs, but its short fangs and small venom volume produce a superficial wound that, while painful, mainly produces swelling in the superficial tissues. It was once thought that the Pygmy Rattler possessed a very potent venom, but its venom is less toxic than that of its cousin, the Massasauga, and no known deaths have occurred as a result of its bite. However, be alert for secondary infections as an aftermath to its bite.

## Copperheads (*Agkistrodon contortrix*): Mildly Dangerous

Copperheads are moderate-sized (22 to 53 inches long), relatively primitive pit vipers of the genus *Agkistrodon*, which also includes the Cottonmouth Moccasin. They are usually handsomely colored snakes whose head has a rather copper-like tinge. Their upper lip and lower jaw is lighter than the coppery top of the head. The background color may be a soft pastel pink, buff, or hazel, with large cross bands of chestnut-brown or reddish brown. These dark-edged cross bands are narrow on the back and much wider on the sides. The underside is pinkish white and has two rows of dark spots like the Cottonmouth. The underpart of the tail has a single row of plates for the first two-thirds of its length, while the remainder of the tail has two rows of plates. While these snakes lack rattles, they do vibrate their tails rapidly, which action may produce a clear buzzing sound if they are on dry leaves or grass. There are several subspecies of Copperheads: The Southern, the Broad-Backed, the Northern, and the Osage Copperhead. While there are differences in color and banding pattern, they retain the basic Copperhead design. Copperheads are also commonly called: Chunkheads, Red Oak Snake, Poplar Leaf Snake, the Dryland Moccasin, the Upland Moccasin, and the White Oak Snake.

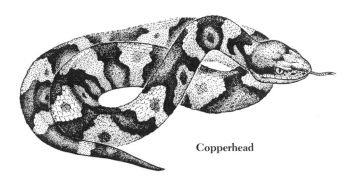

Copperhead

Copperheads are responsible for about one-third of the pit viper bites in the United States, about 2900 a year. For the most part, Copperhead bites are not particularly dangerous. The bites are usually superficial and confined to the deeper layers of the skin, and their poison is the least toxic of the pit vipers. Nonetheless, Copperhead bites do cause a lot of pain and a lot of swelling. These bites, even if untreated, are seldom fatal unless the bite victim is a small child or a very senior citizen. (**Plate 8.**)

**Distribution and Habitat:** Copperheads are found in 30 states, mostly in the eastern two-thirds of the country. Their northern limit is Massachusetts, and they range southward to north Florida and westward to Texas. They live in woody hillsides, mountains, rock piles, and open fields, and under woodpiles and fallen logs. They can be found in both damp and dry forest areas, where they feed on a variety of foods, ranging from frogs to rodents and small birds. They are not particularly aggressive or vicious and will usually try to avoid any human, but, like most snakes, will vigorously defend themselves if they must. They can strike from any position and should be treated with respect. The most bites occurred in North Carolina, 158 bites per million Tar Heels; then came West Virginia, 105 per million, and Arkansas, 93 per 100,000, followed by Oklahoma, Virginia, Texas, Georgia, Kentucky, and Missouri. Bites are rare from November to March and are most frequent in July and August. Sixty-two percent of such bites occur on the ankles and feet, while 36 percent occur on the hands and upper extremities.

**Symptoms:** Pain and considerable swelling of subcutaneous tissues. (see p. 60).

**First Aid:** See p. 63.

**Medical Treatment:** Dr. Findlay Russell recommends a conservative approach to the treatment of Copperhead bites, and suggests holding antivenin unless symptoms indicate severe envenomation or if the victim is either very young or very old.

## Water Moccasins or Cottonmouths
## (*Agistrodon piscivorous*): Dangerous, ☠ Sometimes

The Water Moccasin, *Agkistrodon piscivorous*, is a large, dark colored, banded, thick-bodied pit viper. It has a broad, flat head, distinct neck, and heavily keeled scales. Coloration varies with age. Young are born live, like most pit vipers. These seven- to 13-inch long youngsters are brilliantly colored, with white-edged, rich chocolate-brown bands on a light reddish-brown background, and bright yellow-tipped tails. These young snakes with their vivid markings have fangs and a venom more potent than that of the adult. The adult snake is dark olive brown, and has even darker brown or black cross bands. Its chin and upper lip is yellow or cream-colored, and there is also a yellowish band running from the corner of the mouth to the eye. Very old specimens are uniformly very dark olive to black. These snakes are sometimes called Trap Jaw or Cottonmouths because of their unusual threat

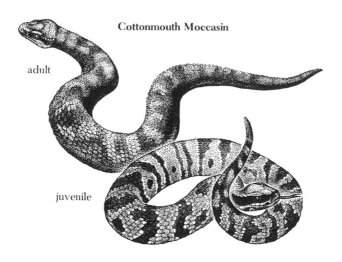

**Cottonmouth Moccasin**

adult

juvenile

display. These pugnacious serpents when disturbed stand their ground and repeatedly gape at any intruder, showing off their conspicuous white mouth parts. During such displays, the snake usually forms a striking coil with its head drawn back and its tail vibrating rapidly. (**Plate 7.**)

Adults are usually three to four feet long, but Moccasins over six feet long have been recorded. Unlike harmless water snakes, the Cottonmouth often swims with its head out of the water, and, contrary to popular belief, cannot strike while in the water—that is, unless you pick it up and provide it with leverage. These snakes are more aggressive than most rattlesnakes, although their venom is less toxic. Being large snakes, they can inject large amounts of venom and thus can produce significant symptoms of envenomation.

**Habitat and Distribution:** Cottonmouths are found only south of the Great Dismal Swamp in Virginia. They range southward to the tip of Florida and westward to southern Illinois, Missouri, and southeastern Oklahoma, and into Texas. There is a small isolated population of Cottonmouths in northern Missouri. It is found in lakes, drainage ditches, lowland swamps, canals, rice fields, ponds, and open flooded flatlands. Cottonmouths are found from sea level to 1500 feet. Some are found on logs or branches over the water, and they will usually drop into the water and swim away if disturbed.

**Symptoms:** Cottonmouth Moccasin bites cause immediate pain, a tremendous amount of swelling, and ecchymosis (black and blue marks).

**First Aid:** See p. 63.

**Medical Treatment:** Antivenin definitely called for; see p. 63.

## Sea Snakes (Hydrophiidae): Can be Dangerous

The family Hydrophiidae contains about 50 species of sea snakes, only one of which is found in the New World. These snakes live by the millions in the Bay of Panama on the Pacific side, and there are no sea snakes in the Atlantic. The Hydrophiidae are closely related to the Elapids but possess an even more deadly neurotoxin; indeed, sea snakes have the most potent venom of any snake. Fortunately, the most aggressive and poisonous members of this family are found in the far eastern

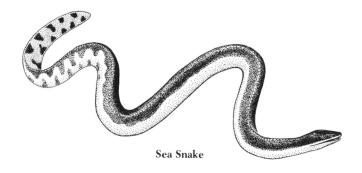

**Sea Snake**

Pacific, and the local representative, while possessed with a very toxic venom, is rather mild-mannered and small.

Sea snakes swim in open seas and are adapted to this form of life. They are superb swimmers, with flattened rudder-like tails. They are air breathers, and their nostrils are located on top of their snouts; hence, they only have to expose the tips of their noses to breathe. They have small belly plates, a gland that desalinates sea water, and a single long, specialized lung that allows them to remain submerged for two or three hours. *Pelamis* has a long flat head, not very much wider than the neck, which is indistinct; indeed, the head is quite eel-like. They vary in color, but one common pattern is yellow with a black or brown stripe down the back. The head is dark, and the laterally flattened wide tail is white with black bars.

**Habitat and Distribution:** *Pelamis* is found from the Gulf of California south into the Gulf of Panama. It may be encountered hundreds of miles out at sea and as deep down as fifty feet, but is mostly found in shallow waters, often floating on the surface. It avoids fresh or brackish waters.

**The Bite:** There has been only one death attributed to the Yellow-Bellied Sea Snake. It is apparently quite docile and usually envenomates only about 40 percent of the time. The venom has several components: a heart poison which can arrest the heart-beat, an anticoagulant, a spreading factor, and—the most active component—a very potent nerve poison that causes paralysis. It only takes ten millionths of a gram of *Pelamis* venom to kill a 20-gram mouse, and less than ten thousandths of a gram to kill a human adult. *Pelamis* has one or more fixed fangs located on each side of the upper jaw. They are short and grooved, hence injecting the venom requires a chewing action.

**Symptoms:** The bite is not painful, only a pinprick, and there are no local symptoms. Many bites are trivial in that they simply cause some muscle pain which goes away in one to three days, but when the snake does envenomate seriously, the symptoms include: muscle pain, thick feeling in tongue, thirst, sweating, and vomiting. Movement of the limbs is difficult and painful. Other symptoms include "lockjaw," drooping of the eyelids, and finally complete paralysis. Death is due to either respiratory or heart failure. Symptoms usually occur within half an hour to an hour and a half after the bite, and fatalities within eight to 24 hours.

**Prevention:** The U.S. Navy Amphibious Forces Manual simply says, "avoid them."

**First Aid:** If you know you have been bitten by a sea snake, put on a constriction band quickly and get to a physician. Incision and suction are not recommended.

**Medical Treatment:** Quickly treat with specific Sea Snake Antivenin, two to four ampoules for trivial symptoms, six to 20 ampoules for severe envenomation. Recovery is usually rapid after antivenin. Other treatment to supplement antivenin can include transfusion, tetanus shot, antibiotic if infection develops; oxygen should be given at first sign of respiratory distress.

# Coral Snakes (Elapidae): Dangerous

Coral Snakes are the only members of the family Elapidae found in the Western Hemisphere and are related to the deadly Old World Cobras and Kraits, which are responsible for thousands of deaths every year. There are several species of Coral Snakes in North and Central America, but only two species are found in the United States, the Eastern Coral Snake, *Micrurus fulvius*, and the Western or Arizona Coral Snake, *Microides euryxanthus*. These snakes are generally small, with the largest Eastern Coral Snake recorded at about four feet, but most are only two or three feet long. They are slender snakes without a distinct neck. They all mount fixed, recurved, grooved fangs in the front of the upper jaw and have moderate-sized venom glands. Unlike the pit viper, which has elliptical pupils, they have round pupils. They are egg layers, usually producing three to twelve eggs in the spring. The

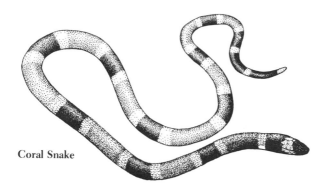

Coral Snake

seven-inch-long young hatch in about three months and look like their parents, having small, blunt heads, and are strikingly marked with vivid rings or red, yellow, and black bands that go all the way around the body. There are some harmless colorful banded species of snakes, but only Coral Snakes have the red and yellowish bands in contact, hence, the old saying, "red on yellow, kill a fellow." (**Plate 1.**)

The Eastern Coral Snake, also called the Harlequin Snake, has a black snout and a broad band of yellow across the head just behind the eyes, followed by a black band, then a thin yellow ring. The tail has only yellow and black rings, while the rest of the body has red, yellow, and black rings. The Arizona Coral Snake differs slightly from its eastern cousin in that the snout and head are black to the angles of the jaws, followed by a yellow band, and then a broad red band. It is more colorful and smaller, averaging only 13 to 21 inches long. There are eight species of Tropical Coral Snakes. They are larger (four to five feet), and not all are brightly banded. In Mexico they are called Coralilla and the "20-minute snake," suggesting the toxicity of its venom. In Central America the Coral Snakes are called Gargantilla, which means necklace.

**Habitat and Distribution:** The Eastern Coral Snake's northern limit is coastal southern parts of North Carolina. Its range extends down the southeast coast all the way to the Florida Keys and westward to southeast Texas and down into Mexico. The Western Coral Snake is found in southern Arizona and southwest New Mexico down into Mexico. The Eastern Coral Snake is found in moist, dense vegetation near streams or ponds in both hardwood and pine forests, where it burrows and is often encountered by persons removing rocks or logs. The Western Coral Snake is found in arroyos and river bottoms, in rocky areas on mountain slopes, and rocky deserts from sea level to almost six thousand feet.

**The Bite and Envenomation:** Despite their small fangs and generally docile nature, Coral Snakes are dangerous because of their highly potent venom. Their fixed fangs are directed backward and curved. When they bite they use a series of chewing motions, thus making several punctures, each of which may or may not have been envenomated. Coral Snakes may envenomate only 60 percent of the bite victims. Most bites occur when someone has picked up the snake. One species actually warns intruders away by forming a coil with its head hidden and its tail raised and forcibly popping its cloacal sac out of its anus with an audible popping sound. Coral snakes account for only one percent of all venomous snake bites.

**Symptoms:** Coral Snake bites produce tiny puncture wounds, two or more, which are minimally painful and cause little or no local swelling. The venom is a potent neurotoxin, and only four or five thousandths of a gram can kill an adult. Symptoms may appear in one to four hours or more, but once they start, deterioration proceeds rapidly. They include blurred vision, droopy eyelids, slurred speech, salivation, drowsiness, giddiness, nausea, vomiting, muscle weakness, difficulty in breathing, reduced heart output, and sometimes burning and prickling sensations of the tongue, mouth, face, fingers, and toes. In severely envenomated cases, shock and heart failure can be terminal. The Eastern Coral Snake is by far the more dangerous snake and should be considered extremely lethal. The Arizona snake is less toxic, bites rarely (only six or so cases reported); hence, treatment will concentrate on the eastern cousin.

**First Aid:** None. Get patient to a physician. Usually a few hours will pass before symptoms occur. Do not give victim food or drink. Keep victim calm. Get medical treatment as quickly as possible.

**Medical Treatment:** Start I.V., three to five vials of Eastern Coral Snake Antivenin (Wyeth Laboratories) as soon as symptoms occur. Coral Snake Antivenin is also prepared in horse serum, hence, be alert for sensitivity reactions. Be prepared to deal with respiratory or cardiac failure.

# Bushmasters (*Lachesis muta*): Very Dangerous

**Description:** The longest American pit viper, the formidable Bushmaster, *Lachesis muta*, is reported to reach a length of twelve feet, but most adults are only eight or nine feet long. This huge serpent has enormous venom glands and very long retractable fangs. Even a six-foot Bushmaster has fangs an inch long. The name *Lachesis* is based on one of the mythical Fates who determined the length of human life. Because of its great length, its strike distance is considerable. While the snake is very long, its girth is not comparable to that of the larger American rattlesnakes. The adult Bushmaster is quite handsome, having a bold pattern of dark diamond-shaped blotches on a gray and brown background.

Unlike other American pit vipers, the Bushmaster lays eggs, and it has been suggested the snake may be particularly aggressive when protecting its nesting area. It is considered to be a bold and very dangerous snake, which has been known to stalk an intruder in its territory. Prior to striking, it often sounds a warning by vibrating its tail back and forth like a rattlesnake, but it lacks a rattle, hence one common name for the snake is "the mute rattler."

**Distribution and Habitat:** The Bushmaster is not particularly abundant and is found only in southern Central America, e.g., Costa Rica and Panama, and its northern limit is Nicaragua. It likes high, dry ground which is well covered with bushes and trees. It is mainly nocturnal and is seldom encountered during daylight hours.

**The Strike:** Like all pit vipers, the Bushmaster has two heat-sensitive pits and can use both heat seeking and vision to strike. The strike may reach more than one-third of the snake's length and is rapid. Its venom is mainly cytotoxic and hemolytic, and drop for drop is quite a bit less toxic than that of the Eastern and Western Diamondback or the Central American Rattlesnake, the Cascabel.

**Prevention, First Aid, and Medical Treatment:** See pages 59 to 65 for a discussion of pit vipers.

# Lanceheaded Vipers (*Bothrops*): Very Dangerous 💀

## *Fer-de-Lances* (Bothrops asper)

**Description:** There are three dozen different species of American lanceheaded pit vipers, all found in the American tropics. The most famous and most dangerous of these is *Bothrops asper* (formerly atrox), whose common name, Fer-de-Lance, originated

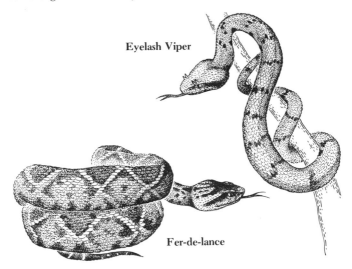

Eyelash Viper

Fer-de-lance

with the French-speaking citizens of the Islands of Martinique and St. Lucia. Another name for this snake is Barba Amarilla, which is Spanish and means "yellow beard." The Fer-de-Lance is a long, slender snake which may attain a maximum length of over eight feet but more usually is only three to four feet long. These snakes are prolific breeders, producing live-born young in litters of 60 to 70, twelve-inch-long newborns that are capable of giving a dangerous bite. As is the case with many pit vipers, the venom of the young snake is more potent than that of adults. Because of its prolific nature, this viper is abundant, and parts of Central America are literally infested with Fer-de-Lance.

The Fer-de-Lance has a narrow neck and a pointed head like the tip of a lance. The body is usually gray-olive brown or gray-green, with conspicuous dark, pale-edged, diamond-shaped blotches. The pattern and color are highly variable. The chin and throat are yellowish, which accounts for its common name, Barba Amarilla, yellow beard. (**Plate 2.**)

**Distribution and Habitat:** Fer-de-Lances are common from southern Mexico through the rest of Central America and can even be found in limited numbers on the islands of Martinique, St. Lucia, Trinidad, and Tobago. They are abundant in low coastal areas of tropical Central America and tend to be present around human settlements where trash and garbage attracts small rodents, mice, and rats, which are their favorite food.

**Plate 1.** *Eastern Coral Snake, p. 80.*

**Plate 2.** *Fer-de-lance, p. 83.*

**Plate 3.** *Eastern Diamondback Rattlesnake, p. 67.*

**Plate 4.** *Western Diamondback Rattlesnake, p. 68.*

**Plate 5.** *Timber Rattlesnake, p. 71.*

**Plate 6.** *Sidewinder, p. 73.*

**Plate 7.** *Cottonmouth Moccasin, p. 77.*

**Plate 8.** *Copperhead, p. 75.*

**Plate 9.** *Massasauga Rattlesnake, p. 74.*

**Plate 10.** *Mojave Rattlesnake, p. 70.*

**Plate 11.** *Crocodile, p. 47.*

**Plate 12.** *Gila Monster, p. 50.*

**Plate 13.** *Scorpion, p. 103.*

**Plate 14.** *Tarantula, p. 101.*

**Plate 15.** *Central American Poisonous Tree Frog, p. 14.*

**Plate 16.** *Central American Poisonous Tree Frog, p. 14.*

**Plate 17.** *Central American Poisonous Tree Frog, p. 14.*

**Plate 18.** *Poisonous Marine Toads, (female on right), p. 15.*

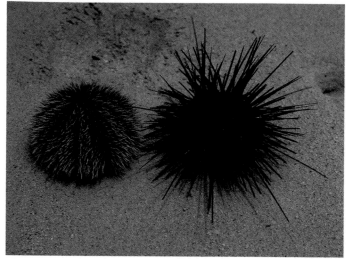

**Plate 19.** *Short-and Long-Spined Sea Urchins, p. 158.*

**Plate 20.** *Fire Worm (Bristle Worm), p. 149.*

**Plate 21.** *Lion's Mane Jellyfish, p. 153.*

**Plate 22.** *Portuguese Man-of-War, p. 151.*

**Plate 23.** *Great White Shark, p. 42.*

**Plate 24.** *Stingray, p. 88.*

**Plate 25.** *Barracuda, p. 33.*

**Plate 26.** *Green Moray Eel, p. 34.*

**Plate 27.** *Stinging Coral (Fire Coral), p. 156.*

**Plate 28.** *Stinging Sponge (Fire Sponge), p. 157.*

**Plate 29.** *Scorpionfish, p. 94.*

**Plate 30.** *Pufferfish, p. 8.*

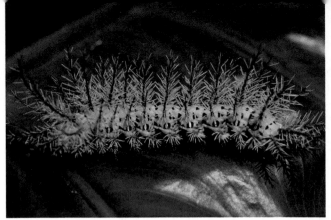

**Plate 31.** *Urticating Caterpillar, p. 134.*

**Plate 32.** *Velvet Ant, p. 124.*

**Plate 33.** *Fire Ants, p. 124.*

These sinister snakes enjoy a very bad reputation because of their large numbers and thus frequent encounters with humans. They have long fangs and large venom glands, and they envenomate with a toxin that destroys red cells and disrupts the walls of blood vessels, causing much hemorrhaging.

**Symptoms:** Pain and swelling around the fang marks usually occurs within minutes. One to three hours later, the swelling spreads and the area around the bite develops extensive blue-black hemorrhages under the skin (ecchymosis) as capillaries ooze blood. This horrifying effect may spread, and even the eyes may become bloodshot.

**First Aid Treatment:** Standard as for all pit vipers.

**Medical Treatment:** Prompt administration of antivenin; see p. 63.

## Other Poisonous Bothrops

There are several other venomous members of the genus *Bothrops* that are numerous in Central America. These include the short (three-foot-long), stout-bodied, very rough-scaled *Bothrops nummifera* or "tommygoff." The tommygoff is also called the "jumping viper," because sometimes when it strikes it literally launches itself into the air and may be able to reach almost twice its length. It is an aggressive snake with large venom glands and is to be respected. It is common in Guatemala, Honduras, and southern Mexico. Another small Lancehead found in the same area is a snouted species, *Bothrops lansbergii*. There are also eight species of greenish, speckled American Lanceheads that have prehensile tails and hang from branches. One of these, "the eyelash viper," *Bothrops schlegelii*, has enlarged scales or horns over its eyes and blends with its arboreal habitat as it hangs in a coiled position ready to strike any passerby. The tails of these prehensile tailed vipers may be red or yellow. While they are small, they do possess a moderately toxic venom and can cause serious damage because they can hit a victim in the face. They are found in forested areas from southernmost Mexico to Panama. (See cover photo.)

## Central American Rattlesnakes (*Crotalus durissus*): Most Dangerous

The Cascabel is one of the largest rattlesnakes, probably reaching lengths of almost six feet and weights of 15 pounds. Because of its large size and extremely powerful venom, it must be considered

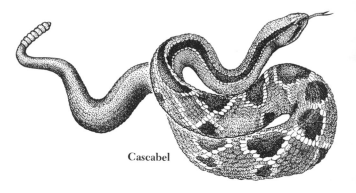

Cascabel

the most dangerous of all rattlesnakes. It has been described as a "sinister and insolent snake" which is known to stand its ground if approached and becomes very aggressive if bothered. This stout, heavy-bodied rattler does not give much warning, sometimes only sounding a click or two with its rattle, which is almost simultaneous with its strike. There are several subspecies of *Crotalus durissus*, all of which have a pair of regular dark stripes separated by a lighter mid-dorsal stripe. The longitudinal line extends from one to four head lengths along the neck.

**Distribution:** *Crotalus durissus*, the Cascabel, is found in southeast Mexico, Guatemala, Honduras, Costa Rica, and El Salvador. Related subspecies are found in southwest and northeast Mexico, as well as the Yucatán. A close relative, *C.d. terrificus*, is found through much of South America.

**Habitat:** Usually ground dwellers, Cascabel prefer dry places and are seldom found on permanently wet ground. They inhabit termite holes and cereal plantations, or farmhouse areas where garbage attracts rodents, their preferred food. They are usually nocturnal, particularly in the heat of summer.

**Prevention:** Wear protective shoes, usually stout mid-calf leather boots, although these large snakes can strike more than two feet and often hit upwards. Wear loose trousers, step on rocks or logs, not over them. Do not put hands into holes or lift rocks or boards with bare hands. (see p. 59).

**Symptoms:** *Crotalus durissus* has a potent venom, containing both neurotoxic and hematoxic components. Shortly after being bitten by a Cascabel, there is intense pain at the site of the bite, often followed by a local sensation of tingling and prickling. Some victims report that they felt as if insects were creeping on their bodies, while others report numbing, as if the region were anesthetized. The most frightening symptoms are paralysis of the eye muscles, drooping of the upper eyelids, double vision and disturbed pupil reflexes, muscular pain, and dizziness. The victims often try to contract the muscles of their forehead in a vain attempt to raise the upper eyelids.

Symptoms of course depend on the amount of venom injected, and about 20 percent of the time rattlesnakes don't inject any venom. If envenomation is severe, early symptoms include agitation, large volumes of urine, prostration, and loss of consciousness.

Later symptoms include dark urine due to breakdown of muscle myoglobin, followed by cessation of urine formation. The hemolytic component of the venom causes breakdown of red cells, thus producing anemia. Clotting is usually not severely disrupted by *C. durissus* venom. Neural effects predominate, and if immediate first aid and medical treatment isn't provided rapidly, a high proportion of bites will result in death due to respiratory failure.

**First Aid:** See general section on first aid for pit viper bite on p. 63.

**Medical Treatment:** See section on treatment of pit viper bites on p. 63.

# PART IV

# *Marine Fishes That Sting*

## Stingrays: Rarely Lethal

The elasmobranch fishes commonly known as the "stingrays" are among the most important venomous ones. They are common in shallow coastal water, but are also found at depths of up to 150 meters. Stingrays are bottom feeders. They burrow into mud and sand to feed on worms, molluscs, and crustaceans. Their teeth are useless other than for crushing hard-shelled fish. Stingrays have a flat body disc (ranging in size from ten cm to a meter or more in diameter), with a protruding slim tail.

The sting mechanism of the ray consists of a striking organ on the dorsal surface of the tail. This organ, one or more pointed, serrated, bony, spiny stingers whose edges are lined with recurved short barbs which tear the flesh as the sting is withdrawn. The sting is enveloped in a thin layer of skin, the sheath. Inside the sheath, along the length of the stinger, are two grooves containing the glandular cells which secrete the venom. The nature of the venom is unknown.

There are a couple of ways of being stung by a ray, the most common of which is stepping on the fish. The fish, as a defensive mechanism, immediately lashes out its tail and stabs the victim in the foot or leg. Injuries to the chest and abdomen are often incurred by diving onto or lying on top of the rays. There are about 1500 cases of stingray injuries reported annually in the United States, and the actual number is probably higher. According to Dr. Findlay E. Russell, of 623 reported sting injuries he studied, 480 were on the foot, ankle, or leg, 104 on the hand or arms and 27 on the chest or abdomen. Dr. Russell also found that almost half of 4000 stingrays examined had lost the sheath and glandular tissue. Thus, many stingray wounds do not involve envenomation.

There are four families of stingrays, the Dasyatidae, the Gymnuridae, the Myliobatidae, and the Urolophodae.

The family Dasyatidae or whip rays have a disc-shaped body

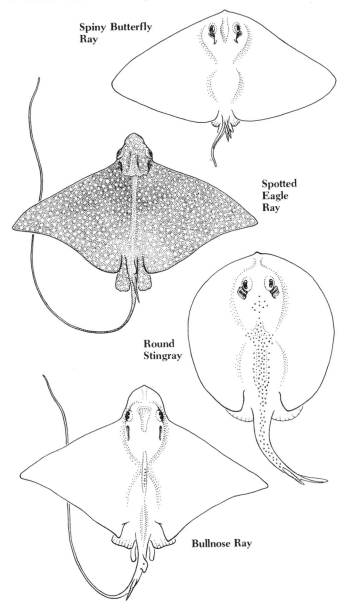

Spiny Butterfly Ray

Spotted Eagle Ray

Round Stingray

Bullnose Ray

with a long, thin, whip-like tail bearing one or more barbed poisonous spines near its base. This stinging apparatus is a potent defensive weapon responsible for a number of wounds to humans. Eleven Dasyatid species are found along the coasts of the United States—seven in the Atlantic, and four in the Pacific. On the Atlantic and Texas coasts, *D. diptururus and D. sabina* are responsible for the most stings.(**Plate 24.**)

The Gymnuridae of "butterfly rays" have short tails and a poorly developed stinging apparatus. They do not constitute a threat to humans.

The Myliobatidae, "bat rays" or spotted "eagle rays," have bird-like extensions of the head and body disc which allow the fish to literally "fly" through the water. These rays have well developed stings, one species, *M. californicus*, is responsible for a number of injuries reported on the west coast of California. *M. californicus* is also noted for its damage to shellfish beds in the San Francisco Bay.

The Urolophodae, or round rays, have a short tail with a well-developed, efficient stinging apparatus. *U. halleri* is probably responsible for the majority of stings reported on the west coast. (See montage of common stingrays on p. 49.)

**Prevention and Control:** The most effective way to avoid being stung while wading is to shuffle your feet along in murky water. This will scare the rays away.

**Symptoms:** The major characteristic of stingray poisoning is immediate intense pain at the site of the injury. The wound may be rather large, jagged and irregular, but often is only a small puncture. If envenomation occurs, the symptoms include: cramping, abdominal pain, nausea and vomiting, respiratory distress, marked vasoconstriction, changes in heart rate, decreased cardiac output, and decreased blood pressure, which in turn may result in respiratory distress, uncoordinated muscular action, confusion, visual impairment, convulsions, and possibly coma. The venom is thought to have a direct effect on human heart muscle.

**First Aid:** A first aid measure which has been found to be very effective is to immerse the wound (if on any extremity) in a hot water bath for 30 to 90 minutes. It is advisable to remove any retained venomous sheath tissue visible in the wound. The hot water should be as hot as the patient can endure. Application of hot compresses to trunk wounds is recommended. It has been found that the venom is a heat-labile protein, so exposure to heat will denature it.

**Medical Treatment:** A victim of a stingray sting is best treated symptomatically. The first thing to do is relieve the pain. Dr. P.J. Mullanney, Director of the Emergency Room at Doctors Hospital in San Diego, California, recommends the following treatment. 30 mg of pentazocine lactate should be given intravenously and the same dose intramuscularly to relieve the pain. Two percent lidocaine should be used on the wound area as a local anesthetic. Debridement (enlargement of wound) should be performed, otherwise large shallow ulcers may form at the site of the injury. Fifty mg of antihistaminic compound administered intramuscularly is recommended, with a prescription of six oral doses of the same. Since the situation is potentially anaphylactic (productive of decreased resistance to action of toxin or drug), an injection of 40 mg of methyl prednisolone sodium succinate is used, and a follow-up prescription of the same on a decreasing dosage schedule for five days. Tetanus prophylaxis and oral analgesics are strongly recommended. Demerol has also been found effective in controlling the pain.

## Ratfishes or Chimaeras (*Hydrolagus collei*): Never Lethal

Ratfish or *Chimaeras* are actually ugly, cartilaginous fish closely related to sharks and rays. They have long, tapered bodies, up to three feet in length, that end in pointed tails. Their metallic silvery iridescent skin is smooth and without scales. Their heads, large and ugly, have a small mouth with a notched upper lip and round protruding snout. The first dorsal fin of these fishes is quite prominent, and its anterior margin is equipped with a sharp-pointed venomous spine. The venom glands are in the skin covering the back of the spine. Being stung by the needle-sharp spine is accidental, and usually happens when removing a fish from the hook. The sting is very painful. Only one species,

Ratfish

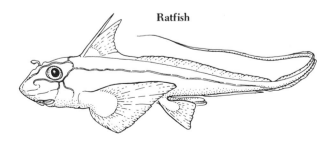

*Hydrolagus colliei*, is worthy of note and that is found only on the Pacific coast.

**Distribution and Habitat:** Ratfish are found in shallow waters down to more than a thousand feet in the Pacific from Alaska to Baja, California. They are frequently encountered off the California coast.

**Prevention:** Recognize the fish and avoid the dorsal spine.

**Symptoms:** Very sharp burning pain, rapid onset. Not much information available on this species.

**First Aid and Medical Treatment:** No information available. Treat as you would a stingray sting.

## True Fishes That Sting

True fish, distinguished from the elasmobranches or cartilaginous fish (sharks and rays), have bony skeletons and belong to the class Osteichthyes. They are a more recent evolutionary development than the cartilaginous fish and inhabit both salt and fresh waters from the Arctic to the Antarctic. They are most usually covered with overlapping bony scales, although some have naked skins. They have a number of bony, rayed fins which are used in locomotion, and in some species the fin rays have evolved into venomous spines capable of inflicting a very painful and sometimes life-threatening sting. Some fish have powerful tooth-lined jaws capable of inflicting a serious bite, and some fish produce or concentrate poisons that make them dangerous to eat.

In the diagram below major anatomical features of fish are shown, in this case in a venomous Sea Catfish. The anterior dorsal or front upper fin is sometimes equipped with a venomous spine

**Anatomy of a fish**

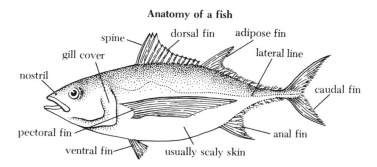

spine · dorsal fin · adipose fin · gill cover · lateral line · nostril · caudal fin · pectoral fin · anal fin · ventral fin · usually scaly skin

in this species. There is a soft posterior dorsal fin, a tail or caudal fin, a single anal fin, a pair of pelvic fins, and a pair of pectoral fins which are sometimes equipped with venomous spines. Fish breathe by means of gills which are internal and covered by a bony operculum or gill cover.

The variety of shapes and colors of fish is enormous, and in this book structural details in the text will be simple and identification will be provided by drawings which in the final analysis are the best means of identification.

## Catfishes (Ictaluridae and Aridae): Never Lethal

There are over 9 thousand species of catfish found in two families, the freshwater catfish, the Ictaluridae, and the marine and brackish-water catfish, the family Aridae. The majority of species are found in fresh water and vary considerably in size and somewhat in shape. Some have small heads, some large heads, some have skin covered in bony plates, but most are clad in a scaleless, tough, glandular, smooth skin that is very slimy to the touch. Catfish derive their name from cat-like whiskers, called barbels, located on the snout, jaw, and chin.

There are two major sea cats found off the East Coast. These are *Bagre marina*, also appropriately called the Gaff Topsail Cat, and the Sea Catfish, *Arius felis*. Both are found from Cape Cod, Massachusetts, to Panama, but are more common in southern harbors and estuaries. The freshwater catfish, including Channel Cats and Bullheads, are widely distributed in ponds and streams and are considered a delicacy by some. They vary considerably in size and shape, but all follow the basic description.

**Venom Apparatus and Sting:** Catfish are equipped with three stinging spines, one located on the leading edge of the first dorsal fin, and the other two on the pectoral fins. The spines are needle-sharp, stout bones sometimes lined with backward-curving teeth.

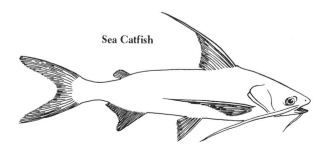

Sea Catfish

The spines are attached to swivel joints, and the catfish can voluntarily erect them. Each spine is covered by skin which contains numerous venom-secreting glands. Those species with toothed spines can produce a very badly lacerated puncture wound.

**Symptoms:** Instant pain is throbbing, and the site of the pain feels burning hot. The pain may radiate and affect the entire arm. The area of the sting initially becomes very pale, but soon turns first blue-purple and then red and swollen. In some cases, the swelling can become quite extensive. The pain may last several hours to two days, and the swelling will usually subside in a day or two. The wound itself is not serious, but sometimes may require a week or two to heal. Bacterial infection of the wound can be a major complication.

**Prevention:** Be very careful handling catfish and avoid the dorsal and pectoral spines.

**First Aid:** Clean the wound thoroughly with soap and water. Local antiseptic may be of help.

**Medical Treatment:** None, but be alert for secondary infection, including gangrene. A tetanus shot is suggested.

## Scorpionfishes (Scorpionidae): Possibly Lethal

The family Scorpionidae includes some of the most venomous fish in the world. Fortunately, the deadly Stone Fish of the Indo-Pacific and the Zebrafish (also called Lionfish or Turkeyfish) are not native to American waters. Although there are quite a few Zebrafish kept in tropical marine aquaria, they will not be discussed in this book. There are native Scorpionfish on both coasts, *Scorpaena guttata*, the California Scorpionfish, and *Scorpaena plumieri* of the Atlantic coast. They are usually small (maximum length, 17 inches), grotesquely ugly fish, usually reddish brown with mottling in various grays, browns, or purples on their upper surface and fins, and pinkish underneath. They have twelve dorsal fin spines, three anal fin spines, and two pelvic fin spines, all of which are pointed and sheathed in skin that contains venom glands. The venom is a complex substance that includes a nerve poison. Their heads have many fleshy projections called cirri. (**Plate 29.**)

According to Dr. F.G. Russell, 80 percent of California Scorpionfish stings occur when fishermen handle the fish. About 300 cases per year are reported in the United States, and the usual site of envenomation is the fingers.

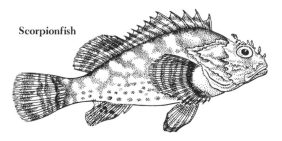

Scorpionfish

**Distribution and Habitat:** Shallow to deep waters off the California coast; particularly numerous off southern California down to Baja, California. Often found around breakwaters or rocky reefs. An Atlantic cousin, *S. plumieri*, is found from Massachusetts to the Caribbean in similar habitat.

**Symptoms:** Dr. Russell has collected a hundred case histories and based his description of "sculpin poisoning" on these cases. At the sting site, there is almost instant intense throbbing pain, which can spread throughout the hand and arm in minutes. The area around the wound becomes pale, and then the finger becomes red and swollen. Some victims become nauseated and vomit, feel weak, sweat, experience bladder urgency, get a headache, and have diarrhea. The injured finger and arm may get numb and the lymph nodes in the armpit swell in about one-third of the cases.

The pain may continue for several hours, but the swelling and tenderness may last for several days. If envenomation is severe, the pain can be agonizing, respiration may become difficult, and the victim may go into shock. In most stings, recovery is complete, and there are no late harmful effects.

**Prevention and Control:** Be careful handling *S. guttata*. Experienced fishermen and bait boys are usually knowledgeable, but when you bring the fish home the person who cleans it might get stung.

**First Aid:** Clean wound and immerse hand in hot water. Otherwise treat as you would a stingray wound.

## Toadfishes (Batrachoididae)

The repulsive, grotesque looking Toadfish, family Batrachoididae, is found in warmer waters of the American coasts. Most are rather small, shy fish that hide in the sand or mud, sometimes

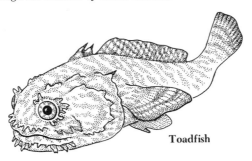

Toadfish

almost completely buried. They also seek out crevices or burrows, or hide among seaweed and rocks. They are masters at blending in with their environment and can change color. They are usually encountered only during the summer months and migrate to deeper waters in the winter.

They have large heads with many fleshy projections, particularly on the lower jaw, plump bellies, and a tapered body. Their stubby anterior dorsal fins have two venomous spines, and there is also a poisonous spine on each gill cover. These spines are hollow and needle-sharp. The venom is produced by glands at the base of the spine and is conducted along the hypodermic-like spine. Their sting produces excruciating, intense pain that radiates into the affected limb, which subsequently becomes swollen, inflamed, and hot.

Stings usually occur when removing them from a hook or when wading in muddy waters. There are several American species: the Oyster Toadfish, *Opsanus tau*, and three others, *Thalassophryne reticulata, T. maculosa,* and *T. dowi.*

**Distribution and Habitat:** Shallow sandy or muddy bottoms. *Opsanus tau* from Massachusetts to the Caribbean, *T. reticulata* and *T. dowi* off the Pacific coast of Central America, and *T. maculosa* off the West Indies.

**Symptoms:** Almost instant pain, sometimes intense, develops rapidly after the victim is stung, followed by redness, swelling, and radiating pain. There is not much available in the literature; hence, details are sketchy. No fatalities have been reported.

**Prevention and Control:** Be very careful handling these fish and wear sneakers when wading in sandy or muddy bottoms.

**First Aid and Treatment:** Same as for stingray stings.

# PART V
# *Arthropods That Envenomate*

## ARACHNIDS (ARACHNIDAE):
## Spiders, Scorpions, Ticks, Chiggers, and Mites

Few creatures are as universally abhorred and unusual as spiders. They evolved over 300 million years ago and are indeed remarkable. They have an external skeleton and eight legs with 56 leg joints, can perform miracles of locomotion, readily moving backwards, forwards, up, down, and sideways. Some are equipped with poisonous fangs, chelicerae, with which to immobilize their prey. Foods are then predigested outside of the body and then sucked into the spider's bowel. Spiders may have as many as a thousand spinning tubes with which they weave webs of varying dimensions, complexity, and sometimes beauty. This webbing is extraordinarily light yet incredibly strong.

Of the 50,000 to 70,000 known species of spiders in North America, only a few are harmful to humans, with only three poisonous spiders posing an actual threat. The chief culprit among them is Latrodectus, the infamous "Black Widow," a shiny black, sedentary, shy creature that only bites in self defense. Although as many as two thousand black widow bites may occur in a year, they account for only a few deaths.

Almost everybody fears spiders. They often occupy our bad dreams. Like Little Miss Muffet, many people have arachniphobia (fear of spiders). Brave men have been sent screaming by a creature they outweigh by some million times. The medieval mass hysteria over fear of the bite of the fuzzy Tarantula gave rise to music and frenzied dance, the tarantella. Actually most Tarantula bites are no worse than bee stings, although there is one Mexican variety of Tarantula that is considered mildly harmful.

Scorpions of the southwestern United States, some Caribbean islands, and Mexico are truly to be feared. The notorious Durango Scorpion of Mexico was responsible for over 1200 deaths per year.

Finally, the real scourge of mankind have been the lesser lights among the arachnids. Ticks, chiggers, and mites have not only caused us itchy days and sleepless nights but have also been the vectors for a number of deadly diseases. Scrub Typhus and Rocky Mountain Spotted Fever are two of the worst ones.

## Black Widow Spiders (*Latrodectus mactans*): Rarely 💀

One of two dangerous species of spiders in the United States and southern Canada is the shiny black female Black Widow. This spider is not aggressive but will bite if mildly provoked or when guarding a nest with an egg sac. She is instantly identifiable by the well-known red hourglass or red dot on the abdomen's underside. The male is small, one-third the size of the female, and although poisonous, has such weak fangs that they cannot pierce human skin. (See cover photo.)

**Habitat:** Dark, moist brush piles, wood stacks, shelters, barns, outhouses (often under the seat). About 50 percent of all bites are on the genitals when the unsuspecting victim sits down, disturbs the spider and is bitten.

**Distribution:** All states except Alaska. Also found in southern Canada, Mexico, and Central America. Most prevalent in warmer climates but also present in cooler environs. Found up to 8000 feet. Most bites occur in June, July, and August. Females hibernate during the winter, and bites are rare during that time. Most fatalities take place in the southeastern United States.

**Avoidance and Control:** Frequent cleaning to remove spiders and their webs from buildings and outdoor living areas will decrease

**Black Widow Spider**

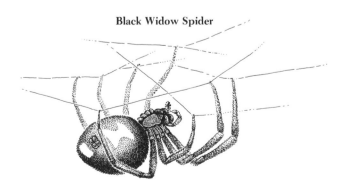

the possibility of accidental bites. Routine hose washings of potential spider habitats, such as privies and wood piles. Removal of habitat and egg sacs may help control the population. Insecticides don't work very well on Black Widows.

**Symptoms:** The initial response to a Black Widow bite is a pinprick wound that is so small that it may be virtually invisible. There is little local reaction, but within 20 to 40 minutes, the bite victim may experience dull pain in the bitten part. Pain spreads to shoulders, chest, back, and abdomen, which may become boardlike in from half an hour to two hours. Nausea, vomiting, headache, hypertension, weakness, increased salivation, inability to lift eyelids, anxiety; in severe envenomation, respiratory difficulties and paralysis. Children and people over 60 or people with high blood pressure or heart disease are considered to be at high risk.

**First Aid:** None. Go to physician or hospital quickly.

**Medical Treatment:** Use muscle relaxants such as Methocarbamol (Robaxin) (10 ml, 100 mg I.V. over 10 minutes). Follow up with another 10 ml in 250 ml saline drip. Diazepam (Valium) is also effective (5 to 10 mg I.V.). To further treat muscle spasm, give 10 ml 10 percent calcium gluconate, but monitor cardiac performance during this treatment. These relaxants will often relieve the pain, but if the pain is severe, narcotic analgesics may be needed. Treatment may have to be repeated at 3- to 4-hour intervals.

In cases showing severe envenomation (shortness of breath and high blood pressure), Lactrodectus Antivenin (Merck-Sharp and Dohme) should be given (1 ampoule in 10 to 50 ml saline I.V.). Watch for allergic reactions to antivenin and be prepared to treat.

## Brown Recluse Spiders (*Loxosceles*): Rarely ☠

There are ten species of dangerous Brown Recluse Spiders in North America and the West Indies, which have been responsible for a small number of deaths. They are also called Violin Spiders because of the unique markings on their backs. Both the male and female are poisonous, but are smaller and less dangerous than the Back Widow. The Brown Recluse is a medium-sized spider with a two- to four-cm (0.8-1.6 in) leg span and a color range from yellowtan to dark brown. The most distinguishing characteristics are six eyes (most spiders have eight eyes) arranged in a semicircle of three pairs on top of the head, and a violin-shaped marking extending from the area of the eyes to the abdomen.

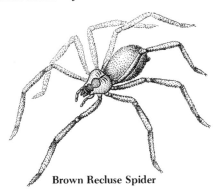

**Brown Recluse Spider**

**Distribution:** Brown recluse spiders occur throughout an area of the southcentral States, including Alabama, Arkansas, Georgia, Illinois, Indiana, Iowa, Kansas, Kentucky, Louisiana, Ohio, Oklahoma, Mississippi, Missouri, Tennessee, and Texas. Localized populations of this spider, probably imported from the southcentral states, have been reported from Arizona, Wyoming, California, Florida, New Jersey, North Carolina, Pennsylvania, and Washington, D.C. Due to the mobility of the United States citizenry, specimens can be easily transported in household goods from the spider's home range in the southcentral United States to any other area of the country. Under favorable conditions, the relocated spiders can survive for an extended period of time and possibly become established.

**Habitat and Behavior:** Within its range, the brown recluse spider will readily establish populations inside parts of buildings which are generally dry, littered, and undisturbed for long periods of time. The spider also can be found outside in protected areas (under rocks and loose bark). Members of this species are nonaggressive and normally attempt to escape whenever they are threatened. Thus, most instances of bites occur when the spider is inadvertently trapped, such as when the victim puts on clothing in which the spider is hiding, steps on a wandering spider at night, or cleans closets or other storage areas where the spider resides.

**Avoidance and Control:** Any of the following actions will help prevent contact with the brown recluse spider: shake out clothing and bedding before use; eliminate collections of papers and unused boxes; throroughly clean beneath and behind furniture; remove spiders, webs, and egg cases from living and storage areas; and properly use appropriate insecticides.

**Bites, Symptoms, Mortality:** The bite itself produces only a mild stinging feeling and is often overlooked. Pain does not usually develop at the site of the bite until two to eight hours after being bitten. This is accompanied by local reddening. A blister develops, surrounded by a ring of inflamed skin. During the development of the damage, the bite is sometimes surrounded by alternating rings of blanching (whitening) and redness like a bullseye. Three to four days later, the blister becomes a firm swelling which can get up to 1.5 cm in diameter. Seven to fourteen days later, the swelling forms into a somewhat large ulcer. In adults this could be combined with fever and chills. Young children and the elderly are also susceptible to pain in the joints, hives, chills, nausea, vomiting, and general disruptions of blood-forming tissue (hemolytic anemia, thrombocytopenia). Blood may appear in the urine and in some cases acute kidney failure. If these symptoms do not occur within a day after the bite, survival prospects are excellent. Only a few fatal cases have been reported.

**First Aid:** Just keep the local wound clean and see a physician.

**Medical Treatment:** There is no antivenin for the tissue toxin of the Brown Recluse. Once diagnosis is certain (it helps to bring in the spider, but the Brown Recluse is a hit-and-run specialist and often gets away). Early corticosteroid therapy may help both local and systemic effects (4 mg dexamethasone injected intramuscularly every six hours during the inflammatory stage).

The ulcer resulting from the bite should be treated conservatively, cleaned each day with peroxide, and soaked three times a day in 1:20 Burrow's solution (10 to 15 minutes). Paint ulcer with triple Aqueous dye. Debride daily. Cover lesion with Telfa and a loose bandage. At bedtime apply polymyxin-bacitracin-neomycin ointment. Healing will occur, but it may take some time.

## Tarantulas (Lycosidae): Never 🕱

There are two species of large, hairy, fierce-looking spiders that are called Tarantulas. The common Tarantula of most of the Southwest is actually a member of the genus *Avicularia*, bird spiders, while the true Tarantulas, genus *Lycosa*, are wolf spiders that migrated northwards. Despite their fearsome appearance, those nocturnal hunters are very gentle; some have even been kept as pets, but if handled roughly they can be provoked to bite. The bite is usually no worse than a wasp sting, but one Central

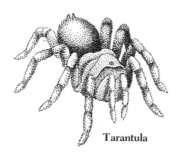

**Tarantula**

American species, *Lycosa phoneutria*, is very aggressive and has a poisonous toxin for which there is now a special antivenin. This red-legged, orange-kneed Tarantula is considered dangerous. (**Plate 14.**)

**The bite:** The Tarantulas have powerful fangs that leave two pinprick-like marks. The mild venom produces only a local inflammation and swelling which lasts only a few hours.

**First Aid:** Treat as a wasp sting. See p. 114.

**Medical Treatment:** None, unless bitten by Red-Legged Tarantula, then see physician.

## Black Jumping Spiders (*Phidippus*): Never Lethal

The most common biting spider in the United States is a small, furry, very aggressive, short-legged, crab-like jumping spider belonging to the genus *Phidippus*. There are several different species. Some have white stripes and "fluorescent" green mouth parts. Because they are slightly hairy, they are often confused with baby Tarantulas. Other species are black with red or orange marks and are mistaken for small Black Widows. These spiders, like most spiders, are very pugnacious, and when they bite hang on tenaciously.

**The Bite:** The bite is sharp and painful, and produces a small wheal (an area of red surrounding a raised pale bump) within minutes.

**Symptoms:** After several minutes, swelling progresses and can be particularly unpleasant if the bite is in an area where the skin is tight (such as a finger joint). The pain is dull and throbbing, and as the pain and swelling subside, there can be considerable itchiness, which may last several days.

**First Aid:** Treat the symptoms as you would an insect sting (see p. 114) and treat local wound.

**Medical Treatment:** None called for other than aspirin and antihistamines; follow instructions on the package.

## Other Spiders That Bite: Never Lethal

There are other spiders that have been reported to bite humans. One is the Running Spider, a pale brown nocturnal hunter common in many thickets in North America. It has no distinctive markings, and its bite causes redness, swelling, and itching, and sometimes causes a small ulcer in the skin. Another biting spider is also brown, has violin-like dorsal markings, and often causes people to mistake it for the truly dangerous Brown Recluse Spider. However, the legs are much heavier than those of the Brown Recluse. Its bite, like that of other poisonous biting spiders, produces local reactions, pain, swelling, and itching. To prevent confusion, it is important that the aggressor be identified to insure proper treatment. Spiders usually hang on for several seconds, and a firm slap kills them. Put the dead spider in a vial of 70 percent alcohol so that it can be identified accurately.

## Scorpions (Scorpionidae): Potentially Lethal

There are about six thousand species of scorpions found throughout the temperate and tropical regions of the world, and most of these are not dangerous. However, in North and Central America

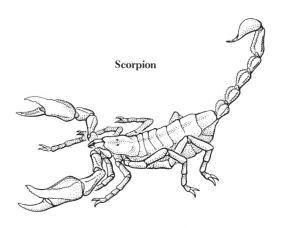

**Scorpion**

there are two potentially deadly species, *Centroides sculpuratus*, found only in Arizona, and *Centroides suffusus*, the lethal "Durango Scorpion" found in western Mexico. Not too many years ago, these Durango Scorpions were responsible for 1500 to 2000 deaths per year, but control measures, education, and provision of better medical treatment have dramatically reduced this number. Less than one percent of *Centroides* stings are lethal to adults, but 25 percent of children under five that are stung will die if untreated.

Scorpions are arachnids; consequently, they have eight legs. The front pair of legs bears crab-like pincers, while the other six are walking legs. The tail of the scorpion has five segments, the last being a bulbous structure containing the venom gland and a very prominent sharp stinger. *Centroides* is a narrow, transparent, midget killer, reaching a maximum size of two inches in length. The *Centroides'* venom is an extremely potent neurotoxin that affects sodium transport in nerve, muscle, and heart cells. The venom also contains a pain-producing substance. (**Plate 13.**)

**Distribution and Habitat:** Arizona and western Mexico. Scorpions like warm to hot, dry climates. They don't like light; consequently, during the day they hide under rocks, bark (indeed *C. sculpuratus* is called the bark scorpion), in crevices under debris, in sleeping bags, clothing, or shoes. Scorpions in general are shy and will sting humans only if disturbed. They hunt by night and, indeed, if you have a black light (ultraviolet) lamp you can see them because they glow when illuminated.

**Envenomation and Symptoms:** Scorpions grasp with their pincers and then bring the tail forward very quickly, driving in the sting and injecting the venom. Upon being stung, there is almost immediate, sharp, burning pain. There is practically no swelling, but numbness, tingling sensations, and shooting pains in the area of the sting are common. The area around the bite becomes very sensitive to touch or temperature change. Young children are at greatest risk, and they may exhibit "roving eye," agitated activity, and high blood pressure. Other symptoms include muscle rigidity, abdominal cramps, loss of control of both bladder and lower bowel, inability to focus the eyes, and spasm of the pharynx.

**Prevention and Control:** Don't pick one off you if it is on your clothes; shake it off. Remove accumulations of debris around camping area. Wear leather gloves when lifting anything off the ground. Wear shoes at night. Shake out sleeping bags, clothing, and shoes before using. Insecticides help, but allow time for them to act, since some cause the scorpion to become hyperactive before dying.

**First Aid:** Do not use narcotics or tranquilizers (aspirin may be helpful). Immediate application of an ice bag may reduce the pain. Do not use a constriction band; do not incise and apply suction. Get victim to a physician for Centroides stings. Other scorpions have less potent venom, and the sting only causes pain and swelling.

**Medical Treatment:** I.V. pentobarbital (15 mg/kg) for agitation. If severe symptoms develop, use Scorpion Antivenin, which in the United States is available only in Arizona. Apply triple antibiotic ointment to wound; administer calcium gluconate 10 ml 10 percent I.V. to control muscle pain. Be prepared to treat shock.

## Ticks (Ixoidae): Can Transmit Lethal Diseases

Ticks belong to the same class of animals as spiders, scorpions, and mites, the class Arachnoidea. They are small, external, blood-sucking parasites found all over the world. They have few natural enemies and a prodigious reproductive capacity; hence they can be very numerous. As adults, they have eight legs that stick out prominently from a flattened, leathery, egg-shaped body. They are capable of becoming quite distended when filled with their host's blood, particularly the females, which are considerably

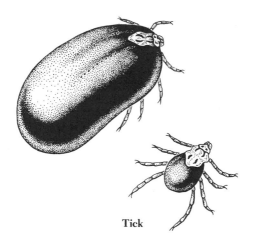

**Tick**

larger than the males. The mouth consists of two small retractile jaws (mandibles), two short appendages called palps, and a central probe equipped with recurved teeth (the hypostome). These structures are attached to a plate called the capitulum. Ticks attach to the host with its mouth parts, which are not only imbedded in the skin but are also glued in place by a cement-like secretion. Sometimes, when pulling off an imbedded tick, the capitulum and its attached parts remain in the skin and cause a local reaction. Ticks can voluntarily detach from the host.

Ticks have sense organs which enable them to detect mammals as much as 25 feet away. They respond to shadows, touch, and odors, and either drop onto or on contact latch onto a passing victim. Once on you, they climb to a comfortable spot, often the head, and imbed their mouth parts and start to suck blood. During this time they inject their saliva, which contains a variety of proteins including anticoagulants and a toxic substance. There are three species of ticks that commonly attack humans: the Lone Star Tick, the American Dog Tick, and the Wood Tick. They are most active between March and August, when they become sexually active. Females will remain attached to their host for from five to 13 days during this period and then detach themselves.

**Distribution and Habitat:** Over much of the United States and Mexico from sea level to high woodlands and meadows below the frost line. They are found on stalks of grasses, weeds, and shrubs as well as trees.

**Prevention and Control:** Standard repellents sprayed on clothing may do some good, but in heavily infested areas you are bound to pick up ticks. Always examine body and clothes and pull them off before they imbed their mouth parts.

**Symptoms:** Ticks can transmit a number of diseases caused by microorganisms such as Rickettsia. They cause Rocky Mountain Fever, Lyme disease, and Q Fever. Their toxin can also cause tick paralysis or tick toxicosis. Tick paralysis has occurred in British Columbia, the northwest United States, and the southeast United States. It is not common, and occurs mostly in children, where it is a potentially fatal disease. The toxin is a nerve poison. Children, most usually female, complain of tingling in the legs and have trouble walking. They become irritable and weak, and lose their appetites. Twenty-four to 48 hours later, there is a rapid progression of sensory disturbances, followed by paralysis, which can be pronounced in the tongue and face. The paralysis may be so severe that respiratory paralysis and death result.

**Treatment:** If symptoms described above occur, make careful search for ticks and remove by painting them with kerosene, nail polish remover, or gasoline. The tick will usually let go.

**Local Reactions:** Days, weeks, or even months after a tick bite, a localized hard, inflamed granuloma may develop. This hard lump may be anywhere from a quarter of an inch to an inch and a half in diameter and may last months before it spontaneously disappears.

## Chigger Mites (Trombidiiae): Never Lethal

Chiggers, also known as "red bugs" or "jiggers," are one of the few of 35,000 species of mites that prey on humans. Like all members of the arachnids, they have eight legs and a pair of piercing jaws or chelicerae. They have a complicated life cycle, and it is only the larval stage that attacks humans. In cooler climates, the larvae are present only in the summer months, but in southern warmer climates (60°F or warmer) they may thrive through most of the year. These larvae are almost at the limits of human vision, being 150th of an inch long when not fed. Chiggers live in dense population islands in grassy fields, meadows, and scrubby savannahs. Often one can sit or stand on such an island and be heavily attacked, while another only a few feet away will not encounter a single chigger. The chigger crawls onto its victim and seeks out a favorite spot, often where clothing is tight or where parts of the body are in contact, e.g., the groin, belt line, ankles, back of the

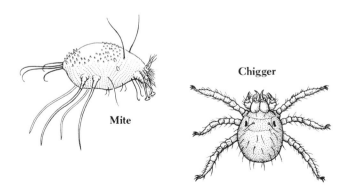

Mite

Chigger

knees, and armpit. It chews into the skin with its chelicerae and injects its saliva, which digests human skin cells, which are then sucked up. As the chigger bores deeper and becomes progressively engorged, a tube called a stylosome is formed. It is the stylosome tube and the body's reaction to it that causes the awful itch.

**Symptoms:** The chigger remains on its victim for three to four days before dropping off of its own will. The itching starts within hours and is worse at night. In the early stages of attack, all you see is an itchy bump with a red pinpoint, the chigger, in its middle. Within a day, it forms an intensely itchy hive with a tiny, fluid-filled, pinhead-size blister in its center. Even after the chigger departs, the lesions and itch persist intermittently for seven to ten days. The chigger sores may be almost an inch in diameter, and look like chicken pox, only they are highly localized.

**Prevention:** Treat both clothing and skin with repellent such as "deet" (see p. 117). Chiggers may remain on clothing for some time, hence, field clothing should be washed in water heated to 100°F.

**First Aid:** Reduce itching with steroid creams and local anesthetic creams available at most drug stores. Try to limit scratching, since it may lead to secondary infection.

**Medical Treatment:** If secondary infection results, consult your physician.

## Itch Mites (Sarcoptidae): Never Lethal

Itch mites are Arachnoidea, belonging to the family Sarcoptidae, are also called sarcoptic itch mites or scabies mites. These whitish skin parasites have a round body, and no distinct head, but do have jaws. They have eight legs, the two front pair equipped with suckers and the rear two pair with long bristles. They are almost invisible to the naked eye, being only 4/10 of a mm long. Females are larger than males and are responsible for scabies itch. The mite is usually acquired by personal contact but can also come from shared living quarters. The female, once on the skin, attaches itself with its suckers, raises its hind end, and eats its way into the skin in 30 to 40 minutes. Once in the skin, the female burrows out a tunnel behind her, where she deposits eggs. This tunneling goes on for about 60 days, at speeds of ¼ to two inches per day, and then she dies. The eggs hatch, and larvae leave the tunnel and move over the skin.

**Symptoms:** The tunneling in its initial stages does not produce itching, but after a month or so, the toxic secretions of the female cause inflammation and intense itching. This itch has been called "the Norwegian itch" or "seven year itch." Apparently the mite is highly selective about where she burrows, preferring (63 percent) webs between fingers and where the wrist flexes, (2 percent) the armpit, (11 percent) the elbows, (9 percent) the feet and ankles, (8 percent) the penis, buttocks and nipple area in adult females.

Diagnosis is based on distribution, symptoms, and detection of the tunnels, which appear as tiny grey or brownish lines in the skin. The secondary stages involve red hives, lumps, and sometimes scabbed-over wounds.

**Distribution:** The mites are very widely distributed worldwide, but can only survive for three days to two weeks in moist, cool air. Their best habitat is human skin. Thus, wherever there are people there can be Itch Mites.

**Prevention and Control:** Be careful about sharing a bed with strangers. There are no really effective control measures.

**First Aid:** None.

**Medical Treatment:** Consult a physician, who will confirm the diagnosis and recommend a scabicidal medication. Some of these medications are mildly toxic, and you should carefully follow instructions.

## Centipedes (Chilopoda)

**Identification:** Centipedes are multisegmented, elongate arthropods with a distinct head and one pair of legs, or appendages, per segment. Size is species dependent, with body length ranging from approximately 2.5 to 25 cm (one to ten inches) or more. The number of legs can, therefore, vary from 15 to 100 pairs or more, depending upon the species.

**Distribution:** The range of centipedes varies with the species; however, these arthropods are most numerous in the southern half of the United States.

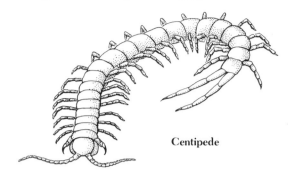

Centipede

**Habitat and Behavior:** Throughout the day, centipedes hide under rocks, boards, or bark, and in cracks, crevices, closets, basements, and other moist, protected locations. At night, they come out of hiding to hunt for prey, which usually consists of insects and other small arthropods. Centipedes inject venom through two powerful claws located on the ventral side of the body immediately behind the head. Contrary to popular belief, centipedes cannot inject venom through their numerous legs. The majority of centipedes found in the United States are small and not a threat to man. Human centipede envenomations occur when a relatively large toxic centipede (*Scolopendra*) is accidentally picked up, stepped on, or otherwise trapped against the body.

**Avoidance and Control:** When camping in a centipede-infested area, carefully invert and shake out sleeping bags, clothes, or other items left in contact with the ground. Always wear shoes when walking about at night, and wear leather gloves when moving rocks or trash from the ground. Usually centipedes are not sufficiently numerous in any one location to warrant chemical control.

**Symptoms:** Almost immediate intense pain is followed in one to four hours by redness, swelling, and burning sensations around the site of the bite, a small two-puncture wound. Sometimes there is swelling of the whole limb. The redness and swelling clears up in four to five hours, and no deaths have been reported.

**First Aid:** Wash with soap and water, apply 10 percent ammonia solution, and apply cool wet dressing of saturated magnesium sulfate solution to the wound. Analgesics such as Tylenol or aspirin may be taken to deal with the pain. Topical pain-killing creams such as benzocaine may lessen local pain.

## Insects (Insecta)

Insects are arthropods, joint-legged animals, that have a tough external skeleton, three distinct body parts (head, thorax, and abdomen), three pairs of legs; most of them have wings. There may be five million species of insects. They range in size from twelve inches down to the size of a dust particle invisible to the naked eye. Insects first appeared on earth about 300 million years ago and have remarkable properties for adapting and surviving. Their tough external skeletons, their flight capabilities, their prodigious reproductive capabilities, and their physiology allow them to endure conditions that would and did destroy other animal species. Some insects can survive temperatures as high as 120°F, while others can handle temperatures as low as minus 30°F. Insects can even tolerate levels of radiation that would be 100 percent lethal for most other animals.

Insect survival is enhanced by a life cycle that goes from egg through a series of larval stages during which there is a gradual change to the adult form (metamorphosis). Some insects undergo a dramatic change in form—complete metamorphosis—which include a pupal stage in a cocoon. If environmental conditions are disadvantageous they may suspend development at one of these stages until conditions improve. Their reproductive capacity is mind-boggling, with some insects capable of laying hundreds of thousands of eggs per mating. The end result is that there are a trillion billion insects in the world, and their weight if added up would be more than ten times the weight of the earth's human population. Considering that the average insect weighs less than a thousandth of an ounce, their numbers are indeed astounding.

Many insects are beneficial to humans, but many are also serious pests that devastate our forests, destroy our crops, and damage stored foods. Other insects are carriers of diseases that have caused millions of human and animal deaths, and some stinging and biting insects which are rarely lethal cause us sleepless, itchy nights and painful bites. This section will concentrate on those families and species that are frequently encountered and either bite or sting. It will include sections on: insecticides, insect repellents, symptoms of stings, and first aid.

Insects are grouped into orders based on common characteristics. The orders are further broken down into families, genera, and species. Sometimes to be able to correctly identify the insect has significant bearing on the treatment; hence, it is essential to know either the scientific or common names of these insect pests.

## A Guide to Insect Anatomy

There are three major anatomical parts of an insect's body, the head, the midpart or thorax, and the segmented abdomen. The head bears a pair of remarkable multifaceted compound eyes that give the insect an almost 360° field of vision. It also is equipped with a pair of chemical-sensing antennae which not only allow the insect to find its prey and mate but also respond to repellents. Last but not least, it has a variety of mouth parts. The insect shown here, the Pestiferous Mosquito, has piercing-sucking mouth parts. All blood-sucking insects have some such mouth parts, and when they attack they insert these mouth parts into the skin and inject their saliva to promote the flow of blood. The saliva contains many substances including enzymes, toxins, and blood vessel dilators. The initial response may or may not be painful, but the subsequent response produces an itchy area of inflammation. Some humans who are sensitized to the insect may experience a life-threatening allergic reaction and can go into shock and die if not treated.

The mid-portion, the thorax, bears three pairs of jointed legs (spiders, ticks, mites, and scorpions have eight legs) and usually one or two pairs of flight wings, although some insects are wingless (e.g., fleas). The hind portion of the body, the abdomen, is segmented, and in sucking insects after a meal of blood can become quite distended. Female insects have specialized egg

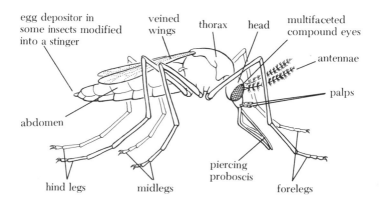

egg depositor in some insects modified into a stinger

veined wings

thorax

head

multifaceted compound eyes

antennae

palps

abdomen

piercing proboscis

hind legs

midlegs

forelegs

depositing appendages at the end of the abdomen. This organ has been modified in stinging insects into a pointed, sharp, hollow stinger which is connected to a venom gland.

## Reactions to Insect Stings: 🐝 Sometimes

**Normal Reactions:** Insect venoms contain a mixture of substances including pain-producing substances (serotonin and kinins), blood vessel dilators (histamines), nerve transmitters (acetylcholine), a spreading factor, enzymes, acids, substances that break down blood cells, and a convulsion factor. The usual response to a sting of wasp or bee is instant and continuing pain and a small red swelling, a wheal, at the site of the sting. The pain and swelling will usually last a few hours and may leave an area that feels hot and itchy. This will also pass in a few more hours and there is no cause for worry. Stings around eyes, nose, and mouth probably cause the most distress, and if stung on the eyelid by a bee, make sure to get the stinger out, since it can cause later complications (see first aid for bee stings). Some people experience exaggerated local reactions that can last a day or more. Multiple stings, a hundred or more, may introduce enough venom to kill a human, although there are cases of people surviving hundreds of bites. When in Kenya I saw two people die from multiple stings when they were attacked by hundreds of very aggressive African honeybees (killer bees). Symptoms of such toxic reactions include diarrhea, vomiting, faintness, convulsions, muscle spasms, panic, and unconsciousness. The cause of death in such cases is cardiovascular collapse, and, as is usually the case, old people or young children are at the greatest risk. A word of caution: when attacked by bees cover your face as much as possible and keep your mouth closed, since stings on the tongue can cause the tongue to swell and you can choke on your own tongue.

**Allergic Reactions:** Most deaths due to bee or wasp sting are due to allergic responses of previously stung hypersensitive individuals. About 30 deaths per year in the United States have been attributed to stinging wasps, hornets, or bees, and some medical people feel the number of actual cases may be twice as high. Anyone who has a known allergy to stinging hymenopterans should always carry an anaphylaxis first aid kit when camping away from medical treatment, because the onset of the allergic reaction can be extremely rapid.

The mildest type of allergic reaction to the proteins in hymenoptera venom is a large local swelling around the sting.

Sometimes this swelling will extend for several inches upstream from the sting, between the sting area and the heart. Such a response is a warning which may indicate a potential anaphylactic reaction. Anaphylactic reactions involve the immune system and can have widespread effects throughout the body, due to the release of our own histamine and histamine-like substances. Histamine is a potent substance that relaxes the muscle in blood vessels, which then expand. This can cause a severe drop in blood pressure; not enough blood reaches critical organs such as the brain; and the victim can collapse, go into a coma, and die. Histamine can also cause rapid onset of swelling of the larynx, lips, and mouth. The sting victim complains, "my throat is closing." The air passageways can become obstructed, and the lips and fingernails turn blue as insufficient oxygen reaches the lungs. This is a grave sign, requiring immediate treatment. Another generalized response by a hypersensitive individual is acute bronchial asthma. The air tubes (bronchi and bronchioles) swell and become obstructed. Onset can be very rapid and the victim may experience difficulty in breathing, wheezing, shortness of breath, pallor, and panic.

The overall anaphylactic response sees a rapid progression of symptoms: the eyes water and become itchy; the inside of the ears may become itchy; the nose runny, stuffy, and irritated, accompanied by sneezing, coughing, wheezing, and shortness of breath; eyes, lips, mouth, and fingers may swell to alarming proportions. Hives, large itchy swollen wheals on the skin, may erupt all over the body. Exhaling may become difficult and wheezing sounds can be heard during exhalation; lips and finger- and toenails appear purple, blood pressure drops, and there is a loss of consciousness, coma, and death. Anaphylaxis must be treated as a medical emergency. With adequate treatment, chances of survival are very good.

## Delayed Reactions to Bee and Wasp Stings

Some bee or wasp sting victims show a series of delayed symptoms ten to fourteen days after being stung. These symptoms include fever, a general sick feeling, headache, hives, joint pains and lymphadenopathy. Such delayed reactions can lead to anaphylactic shock.

### First Aid Treatment for Bee and Wasp Stings:

1. In bee stings, the venom sac and stinger will usually remain imbedded in the skin. The sac continues muscular contraction

introducing more venom unless quickly removed. Do not pull out with a pair of tweezers or fingernails. This squeezes in more venom. Scrape off the stinger with a knife blade or fingernail.

2. Wasps, hornets, and velvet ants do not leave their stingers behind, but their stingers can cause infection hours or days later. Wash off all stings with soap and water and be alert for signs of infection.

3. Elevate and rest stung extremity and apply ice pack to reduce intensity of the pain and the duration of the swelling. Some medical people think a soak in 10 percent ammonia solution or application of a baking soda and water paste may relieve the pain and swelling, but these treatments' value may be only psychosomatic.

4. Oral antihistamines may be helpful in exaggerated local reactions, as will topical steroid creams.

5. People with known allergies should wear a medi-alert bracelet or tag.

## Medical Treatment for Allergic Reactions and Anaphylaxis

Treat mild respiratory problems with oral ephedrine or ephedrine inhaler every two minutes till breathing is normal. Oral antihistamines are also called for. Sensitive individuals should carry the above with them when hiking or camping away from medical care. medical care.

Severe reactions require immediate deep subcutaneous injection—0.3 to 0.5 cc of 1:1000 aqueous epinephrine (children half as much)—and if symptoms indicate, repeat in 15 or 20 minutes. Give Aminophylline by slow I.V. if bronchial spasm develops. Steroids by I.V. drip can be given to supplement the epinephrine and aminophylline. Have oxygen ready and be prepared to treat for shock and cardiovascular collapse. Insect sting kits for early treatment of sting emergency are available from: Center Laboratories, Port Washington, New York (516-767-1873).

**Prevention and Control:** The best way to avoid hymenoptera stings is to prevent human contact with these insects. This is especially important for persons hypersensitive to bee venom. Some preventive steps are:

1. Avoid outdoor activities in unfamiliar areas where stinging insects are known to occur.

2. When outdoors, don't use floral-scented cosmetic products or

leave sweet beverages or foods exposed in areas where they might attract bees.

3. Avoid garbage collection areas, which attract hymenoptera.

4. When outdoors, always wear shoes and, if possible, a long-sleeved shirt, long pants, or other protective clothing. Don't wear clothing with a bright floral print or loose-fitting clothing in which stinging insects may be trapped.

5. Don't make rapid movements around stinging insects or intentionally disturb either the insects or their nests.

6. Eliminate all hymenoptera nests around inhabited areas (wild honey-bee colonies may be removed by a local beekeeper). When necessary, an insecticide such as 5 percent carbaryl dust may be applied in a nesting area within a building to eliminate the nuisance colony.

7. Educate young children on the hazards of venomous arthropods.

8. Hypersensitive individuals can achieve some degree of protection from allergic reactions by getting repeated injections of a weakened extract made from whole bee bodies and bee venom. However, such desensitization treatment does not guarantee immunity, and one recent study reported that 40 percent of desensitized people still exhibited allergic responses to bee stings.

**First Aid and Medical Treatment:** See P. 114.

## Insect Repellents

Early in the 1930s, it was discovered that the chemical ethyl hexanediol was effective in repelling a number of biting-sucking insects and arachnids. This substance is still in use in the commercially available repellent 6-12. An even more potent repellent, N, N, diethyl-meta toluamide, was discovered in the 1950's, and this substance, commonly called "deet," is used in most present-day repellents. It is effective against chiggers, ticks, fleas, mosquitos, and biting-sucking flies, but affords no protection from stinging ants, wasps, bees, or hornets. According to the U.S. Army, the Department of Agriculture, and the Environmental Protection Agency, "deet" is both effective and non-toxic except in some rare individuals with certain genetic metabolic diseases. It can, however, sting when it gets in the eyes or mouth, or onto cuts or rashes. Repellents may be applied as a spray (either hand pump or aerosol), as a solution, as a stick, or as a cream. Towelettes are also available, but they are wasteful, since each towelette can cover only a small area.

According to Consumer Reports (June 1982), not all repellents contain equal amounts of "deet"; hence they vary in effectiveness. Muskol has the most, 95 percent, followed by Repel (52 percent), Cutters (31 percent), Deepwoods Off (29 percent), Off (19 percent), and 6-12 (10 percent, but it also has ethyl hexanediol). The most economical and easily carried forms of repellent are the liquids and creams. Follow instructions carefully, and when in heavily infested areas cover exposed skin areas and spray clothing, since many insects can bite right through fabric.

## Insecticides

There are many kinds of pesticides which can be applied in different forms and in different ways to deal with different pests. *Surface sprays* which leave a deposit of poison when they dry are available in aerosol spray cans or in hand pump sprayers. Some of these are oil based-insecticides and may dissolve or discolor plastics or stain synthetic fibers. There are also *space sprays*, which are released into the air as a fine mist or fog, that are quite effective against flying insects (mosquitoes, flies), but when releasing make sure that any eating utensils or food is covered up to prevent contamination. There are also *insecticidal dusts* available for surface application, and these are good for getting at pests that hide in cracks or other difficult-to-reach places.

Insecticides have common names and generic chemical names. Some of the more common pesticides are lised below in a table from the U.S. Department of Agriculture, Bulletin #96.

## *Insecticide Treatments According to Pest:*

ANTS: Spray nests with mixture containing diazinon, lindane, malathion, or propoxur.

FLEAS: Dust with a mixture of 5% malathion or 5% methoxychlor. Dust or powder can be rubbed into fur of pets safely.

FLIES: Screens, netting, aerosol space sprays.

MITES: Use repellent "deet."

MOSQUITOES: Space spray for flying insects, repellents.

SCORPIONS: Spray nesting areas with surface sprays containing lindane. Watch out, because the initial response may be an excited scorpion.

SPIDERS: Sprays generally ineffective, lindane may have some small effect.

TICKS: For ticks in camp site, cottage, or tent, spray with lindane, malathion, or diazinon.

WASPS: Treat nest after dark with minimal light. Pour liquid
insecticide into holes and cover with moist dirt. Hanging
nests can be hit with special high potency wasp-hornet spray
cans that shoot a stream of poison into the opening.

BEDBUGS: Spray hiding places with lindane, malathion, ronnel,
and pyrethrum (do not use on sleeping bags or mattresses).

## Hymenoptera: ☠ 30 per year

The Hymenoptera is an order of insects whose members have two
pairs of membranous wings and one pair of antennae, and whose
female ovipositor has evolved into a very potent stinging apparatus. Included in this order are several species that can inflict
extremely painful stings: wasps, hornets, bees, the velvet ants,
harvester ants, and the vicious fire ants. Several million people
are stung every year, and while in most cases such stings are
merely a painful nuisance with no prolonged effects, there are
some people who, when stung, experience life threatening
medical emergencies or death. According to the Bureau of Vital
Statistics, more than 30 deaths per year are due to hymenopteran
stings, and of 460 deaths in the United States attributed to
venomous animals between 1950 and 1959, more than half were
caused by Hymenoptera. In the following section the more
common members of this order will be reviewed.

## Bees: Potentially Lethal

Bees are among the world's most beneficial insects, and are the
most important pollinators of plants from the Arctic to the
Equator. Bees also provide humans with honey and beeswax, but
they can inflict painful and sometimes lethal stings. Stinging bees
all belong to the family Apidae, which includes both solitary and
social species. Bees generally are covered by fine feathery hairs,
particularly on the legs and abdomen. While bees have biting
jaws, they don't use them when feeding, since they get most of
their nutrients by lapping up flower nectar. Most common species
of bees have yellow and black stripes on their abdomens and are
most active in the months that plants flower.

**The Stinging Apparatus:** The bee's stinger is retractible and
hidden in a sheath inside the abdomen until it is brought out just
as the bee stings. The stinger is about one-tenth of an inch long
and is composed of three parts which surround the poison canal.
One part, the director, guides two lancets which move up and

down by muscular action. All three parts are barbed and are driven into the flesh. Poison glands in the abdomen are squeezed by the up and down movements of the lancets; thus the venom is forced into the wound. The barbed lancets remain firmly imbedded into the skin, and when the bee flies or is swatted off, the director, lancets, and poison gland are left behind, still injecting poison. Any attempt to pull the sting apparatus out will cause greater injection of venom; hence the stinger must be scraped off with a knife or fingernail (see first aid section on p. 114).

Bee venom contains several biologically active toxic compounds, most of which were described in the Introduction to Hymenoptera, but one deserves particular mention, that being MCD, a peptide that releases the body's own histamine. MCD is the chief product of bee venom and produces pain, dilation of blood vessels, and other allergic type reactions. Another toxin, Apamin, is a nerve poison which can cause muscle spasms and convulsions.

## Solitary Bees

Solitary bees, as their name implies, live alone. Each female builds a nest in a particular habitat, provisions them, lays her eggs, and leaves the larvae to develop on their own. The Large Carpenter Bee hollows out tunnels in wood, usually in the pithy stems of bushes. She is about an inch long, is robust like a bumblebee, and has a naked or hairless abdomen. Her smaller cousin, the Small Carpenter Bee, is only one-fifth of an inch long, is dark-blue-green, and has similar tunneling habits. Other solitary bees include the Mason Bee, the Miner Bee, and the Leafcutter Bee. All have stingers and can trigger allergic reactions in sensitive individuals.

## Honey Bees (Apis mellifera)

The common honeybees, *Apis mellifera*, are true social bees. They are found in the wild and have been domesticated and bred for their pollinating skills and for their production of honey and beeswax. All of these commercial bees in the United States and Canada were imported; they are separated into several races, with the gold Italian and the black and gray Caucasian races making up the majority of bees in the United States. These bees are responsible for the most stings and deaths. In one recent five-year study, Hutchins reported that of 215 reported deaths caused by venomous animals, 52 were caused by bee stings.

Honeybees are highly social insects whose colonies consists of

Bumblebee

an egg-laying queen bee, many male drones, and very large numbers (thousands) of sterile female worker bees who care for the queen, gather food, and care for the young. Honeybees can release "alarm odors" when stinging, and this may attract other bees to the odor-marked victim, thus producing multiple stings. This alarm odor may also increase aggressiveness. Alarm odors may also account for the group aggressive behavior and multiple stings seen when a nest is disturbed.

## Bumblebees (Bombus)

Bumblebees are considered to be relatively primitive social bees. Their colonies lack much of the structure and highly evolved behavior of the honeybees; however, like the honeybees, the bumblebees are diurnal plant feeders and important pollinators of crops. A typical colony consists of at least one queen, several males, and numerous workers. Only young fertilized queens survive the winter to establish new colonies the next spring. The nests are normally located deep in undisturbed ground, like fence rows, and are supplied with a mixture of pollen and honey. During late summer, a colony usually contains between 100 and 500 bees. Although bumblebees are two to three times larger than honeybees, they are neither as aggressive nor as abundant as honeybees, and therefore not as dangerous, but they do produce a fearsome loud buzzing noise as they fly and thus wage psychological warfare.

## Wasps and Hornets: Potentially Lethal

Most wasps have slender bodies composed of three distinct body parts. The mid-part, the thorax, bears two pairs of wings, the anterior pair usually being larger than the rear pair. One family, the Mutillidae or Velvet Ants, are wingless and covered with bright red or orange velvety hairs, while the other family, the Vespidae, have tiny smooth hairs and are typically yellow and black, white and black, dark brown, or steely blue. The wasp abdomen is egg-shaped and attached to the thorax by a very slender stalk; hence, the term "wasp-waisted" for women with very thin waists. Through this inelastic narrow stalk run the digestive tube, blood vessels, and nerves, and because of this constriction, wasps can eat only liquid foods.

Only female wasps and hornets have stingers, and these are generally larger and sharper than bee stingers and they lack barbs; thus the wasp can voluntarily remove its stinger and sting again. Venom is injected by contraction of muscles surrounding the venom sac. Wasps also have strong jaws—mandibles—and are capable of both biting and stinging. Since many wasps are scavengers, the bite can be a source of infection.

Wasps, like bees, can be divided into solitary and social types.

## Solitary Wasps

Among the largest and most beneficial wasps are the solitary forms that prey on a variety of insect pests. These solitary hunters paralyze their prey and carry them to their nests, where they lay an egg and provide the developing larvae with enough food to carry them through development. The largest of the solitary hunter wasps is the Tarantula Hawk, of Mexico and the southwest United States. This large, steely blue-black predator provides its young with tarantulas. There are Mason or Potter Wasps that make jug-shaped mud nests, Digger Wasps that make nests in the ground, and the common, long-waisted, brown Mud Dauber Wasp that sticks mud nests on walls, rocks, or other protected sunny areas. These nests are tubular cells, and the mud dauber fills six to 20 tubes with 20 paralyzed immature spiders to feed her developing young, which emerge as adult wasps in about three weeks. Another common large hunter wasp is the Cicada Killer. Adults emerge in early summer after overwintering as resting larvae. The adult female mates, and then digs a long tunnel in the ground. Then she goes hunting, stinging and paralyzing one or two cicadas, which she drags into the tunnel. She lays a single egg, seals it up with its still-living source of food for her offspring (thus forming a cell), and flies off to find more cicadas. A completed tunnel may contain up to 16 cells. These large solitary wasps are highly selective in their prey and will only sting humans by accident; not so with their more aggressive brethren, the social wasps.

## The Social Wasps (Vespidae)

There are four common species of social wasps that humans encounter frequently. These are the Yellow Jackets, Bald-Faced Hornets, European Hornets, and Paper Wasps. These social wasps are generally considered dangerous because of their large numbers, nesting habits, and very aggressive behavior. They all chew up framents of wood and leaves, which they mix with their own saliva to make a form of paper used in constructing their nests. These nests may be built underground or in the open, attached to branches or projecting eaves of cabins or houses. The nests have several layers of six-sided paper chambers covered by several layers of paper. Usually there is only one entrance-exit opening. Open nests are usually spherical. Queen wasps lay eggs in each cell, and the larvae are fed on insects collected by worker wasps. If their nests are disturbed, social wasps pour out in large numbers to attack the intruder.

## Yellow Jackets (Vespula pennsylvania)

Many a barbecue or picnic has been disrupted by these very aggressive stinging pests called Yellow Jackets. These black-faced wasps have yellow and black stripes and are about two-thirds of an inch in length. While some make paper nests that hang from shrubs or trees, others make their nests in hollows of trees, walls, or even in gopher holes. They are attracted to sweet drinks, food, and bright colors, are very persistent and bold, and have nasty dispositions. They bite and sting without much provocation, and can be downright fearsome if their nest is disturbed. A Yellow Jacket queen can produce 1500 eggs per laying, and these mature into workers in about 30 days, whereupon the queen starts another brood. Thus, a large nest may house a few thousand Yellow Jackets.

## Hornets (Vespa)—The Bald-Faced Hornet (Vespula maculata)

The other dangerous paper-wasp found in North America is the Bald-Faced Hornet, *Vespula maculata*, and its smaller east coast cousin, the European Hornet. These large, bald-faced, black and yellow-white hornets build football-shaped nests that hang from trees. Such nests are often encountered at the forest edge. The European hornet nests in hollow trees or on the sides of cabins. Unlike yellow jackets, hornets usually leave people alone. How-

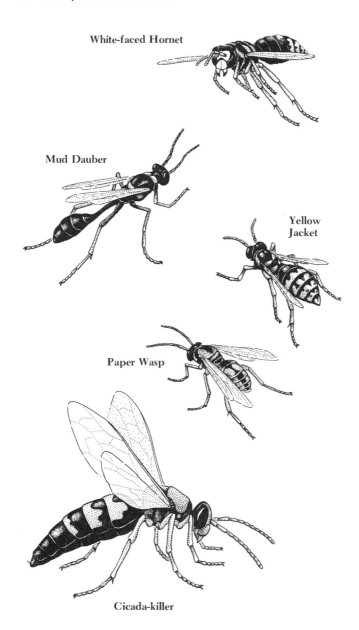

White-faced Hornet

Mud Dauber

Yellow Jacket

Paper Wasp

Cicada-killer

ever, if their nest is disturbed, they become very aggressive and swarm at the intruder, inflicting multiple painful stings. A large nest may contain two to three thousand hornets.

## Polistes Wasps

Polistes are long, slender, reddish-brown wasps which make their nests in cabins, summer houses, and attics, where they winter over. They are not as prolific as yellow jackets or hornets, but a paper wasp nest may contain several hundred larvae, which hibernate over winter and emerge from their honeycomb paper nests inside the house. The paper wasps are more of a nuisance than a threat, since they are relatively mild-mannered, sting only if provoked, and when they do sting it is not as painful as the stings of yellow jackets or hornets. See montage of wasp types.

## Velvet Ants (Mutillidae)

The Velvet Ants of the family Mutillidae are not ants at all, but are furry solitary wasps. The larger males have wings, while the female is wingless. However, she does have a formidable stinger with which she can inflict very painful stings. Velvet ants are also called cow killers, mule killers or woolly ants. They are about a half-inch to an inch long and are covered with bright orange, red, or yellow hairs. They have very thick external skeletons, which provide protection as they run about in search of egg-laying sites. They are most common in the southern and western United States, but one species is commonly found on sandy beaches of Lake Erie during the summer months and causes barefoot bathers considerable pain. They normally sting only when stepped upon or touched by accident. (**Plate 32.**)

## Ants (Formicidae): Seldom Lethal

Ants like the bees and wasps, are hymenopterans, having a constricted waist; the females are equipped with stinging apparatuses. Their antennae are elbowed and sterile workers are wingless. There are two types of American ants that can inflict painful stings and cause harm. These are the imported fire ants and the harvester ants.

## Fire Ants

In 1918, the South American Black Fire Ant, *Solenopsis richteri*, established a beachhead in the United States, and in 1940 its

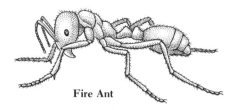

Fire Ant

cousin, the Red Fire Ant, *Solenopsis invicta,* was introduced. Now these ferocious tiny pests are well established in nine Southern states, infesting over 150 million acres. They are highly industrious, well-disciplined social insects that bite and sting. They are tiny—only one-fifth of an inch long—but very aggressive pests nonetheless. Often they latch on with their jaws and pivot, stinging repeatedly. Their nests are made in the ground and are easily identified as elevated earthen mounds 18 to 36 inches in diameter and 3 to 36 inches high, surrounded by undisturbed vegetation. These ants are extraordinarily prolific, and a single acre can hold more than a hundred nests containing as many as 25,000 workers. If their nest is disturbed, they suddenly pour out of the entrance by the thousands and attack with ferocity. The suddenness of this massed onslaught may be triggered by some chemical alarm odor. The end result is that a victim may receive several thousand stings. These immigrant invaders also cause significant agricultural damage and attack luckless domestic animals and pets. (**Plate 33.**)

**Distribution:** Southeastern United States, Alabama, Arkansas, Florida, Georgia, Louisiana, Mississippi, Texas, and the Carolinas.

**Symptoms:** The fire ant toxin is quite potent and produces both immediate and delayed effects. Initially, the sting causes immediate, severe, burning pain which may last several minutes; then the pain subsides and a localized raised wheal forms, expands, and develops into tiny, fluid-filled, raised blisters. Ten hours later, these blisters flatten out and become filled with pus, and these swollen, painful pustules may last several days before being absorbed and replaced by scar tissue. There may be residual effects, such as pigmented areas or two- to three-mm raised scars, persisting for weeks. More fire ant stings are on the legs.

Some people who have a history of allergies and may have been stung previously become sensitized to fire ant venom. These people can have a generalized systemic reaction and may go into anaphylactic shock and die. Some fire ant-caused deaths have been reported.

**First Aid:** Wash with soap and water, apply ice packs or cold compresses, and apply a paste made of baking soda and water.

**Medical Treatment:** For systemic reactions: epinephrine (1:1000) subcutaneously, 0.5 cc for large adult, 0.1 to 0.3 cc for children. Repeat in 5 to 10 minutes if necessary. Antihistamine intramuscularly, 50 mg for an adult, and oral antihistaminics. Be prepared to treat for anaphylactic shock.

## *Harvester Ants* (Pogonomyrmex)

There are several species of stinging harvester ants of the genus *Pogonomyrmex:* The Florida Harvester Ant, the Red Harvester Ant, the Western Harvester Ant, and the California Harvester Ant. These diurnal, soil-inhabiting ants form large colonies of several thousand individuals. Their nests are only slightly raised mounds in dry warm or sandy places. Each nest is surrounded by an area completely cleared of vegetation that can be up to ten feet in diameter. These red or black ants are three times larger than fire ants and are equipped with powerful jaws used to grind seed. When their nest is disturbed, they pour out and attack the intruder in waves, stinging viciously. Small animals have been killed, and humans who have experienced multiple stings have had severe generalized reactions.

**Distribution:** Only the Florida Fire Ant, *P. badius,* is found east of the Mississippi throughout the Southeast, while other harvester ants are all found in localized populations west of the Mississippi.

**Symptoms:** Similar to those of fire ants.

**First Aid:** See fire ants.

**Medical Treatment:** See fire ants.

**Harvester Ant**

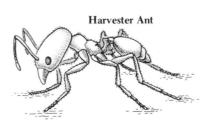

## Diptera: Flies, Mosquitoes, Gnats, and Midges

Of all animals that cause human pain, disease, suffering, and death, none can even come close to the order of insects known as the Diptera. The Diptera, as their name implies, have only two transparent wings, the front pair. The hind wings have evolved into small knoblike balancing organs called halteres. There are 17,000 species of Diptera in North America, and they are very widespread, ranging from just below the Artic Circle southward to the Panama Canal. Some are beneficial, but others take their toll in blood, painful bites, itchy welts, sleepless nights, and disrupted vacations. Some Diptera also transmit debilitating and lethal diseases. The Diptera discussed in this book are all equipped with piercing-sucking mouth parts and are blood suckers. They are: the biting flies, gnats, sand flies, midges, and mosquitoes.

### *Black Flies (Simuliidae)*

Black Flies, also called Turkey Gnats because they transmit parasites to turkeys, or Buffalo Gnats because of their hump-backed appearance, belong to the family Simuliidae. Seventy-five species of these tiny (about three-mm-long), stout-bodied daylight hunters are found in the United States, Canada, and Mexico. Although commonly called Black Flies, their color ranges from black to grey to yellow. They have broad, short wings, and the females have blade-like jaws and piercing stylets with which they can suck blood. These vicious little blood suckers stab their bayonet-like mouth parts into the skin and inject their salivary juices, which may contain a numbing local anesthetic. Thus, when they first bite, all that can be seen is a small drop of blood, but as the local anesthetic wears off, a very intensely painful, extremely itchy lump forms on the skin.

Black Flies breed by the millions wherever there is running

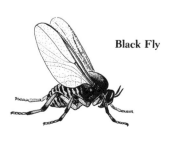

**Black Fly**

water. Swarms of adult females attack persistently, even following their victims for several miles. They literally form a cloud as they attack en masse. They concentrate their attack on eyes, ears, nostrils, wrists, and knees. There have been reports of extreme panic reactions to the attack of a Black Fly swarm, and some sensitized individuals have gone into anaphylactic shock after being repeatedly bitten.

**Distribution and Habitat:** Females lay egg clusters on sticks, rocks, or plants below the surface of running water. The eggs hatch in several days and form aquatic larvae, which later emerge as adults. They are widespread in the northern states and Canada, but can also be found in Mexico and Central America in isolated areas near water. They are most numerous in early summer, and numbers decline in early September.

**Symptoms:** The initial bite is often painless, but may leave a small drop of blood. Within an hour a very painful, itchy wheal forms, which may last several days. Later these bites may form blister-like lumps or hard pus-filled lumps that may last for weeks or even months. Deaths are rare, but have been reported.

In Central America and elsewhere in the world, Simulid Flies transmit a parasitic worm infection, onchocerciasis, that eventually causes blindness. In Africa, millions of people have been blinded, but Canadian and American simulids do not cause river blindness.

**Prevention and Control:** Space sprays or foggers can provide temporary protection of a camp site, and repellents like "deet" also provide individual protection for several hours. Mechanical protection, gloves, long sleeves, and long trousers prevent bites. Brimmed hats fitted with very fine mesh and sprayed with "deet" will keep the little bugs away from your eye, nostrils, and ears. They are attracted to light. Thus, use red rather than white lights at camp sites.

**First Aid Treatment:** Wash with soap and water, and when itch starts use anesthetic creams containing benzocaine. Soothing lotions such as calamine may also help. Oral antihistaminics may help control the itching. Scratching can produce secondary infection, so if the skin is broken use a topical antiseptic.

**Medical Treatment:** None. Be alert for anaphylaxis or toxic reactions and treat symptomatically.

Punkie

## Biting Midges and Gnats *(Ceratopogonidae)*

Tiny mosquito-like flies of the family Ceratopogonidae are night-time pests that swarm in vast numbers as the sun goes down. They have common names like "punkies," "no-see-ums," "midges," and gnats. They are tiny (one to three mm), and often can penetrate even very fine screening. While they bite viciously, the discomfort produced is much less severe than the bites of Black Flies.

**Distribution and Habitat:** Around water, moist woods of the Atlantic coast and northern and Canadian woodlands. They gather in swarms or clouds at night.

**Symptoms:** Raised itchy but not particularly painful lumps last several hours, but some victims may show delayed responses of round, elevated, pus-filled blisters that last a few days.

**Prevention:** Space foggers afford temporary protection at a campsite. Repellents do work, and protective clothing is a must. Spray repellent on screens and tent netting.

**First Aid and Medical Treatment:** Same as for any biting-sucking fly or mosquito.

## Sand Flies (Phlebotomus)

The fly family Psychodidae, genus *Phlebotomus*, are tiny, hairy, blood-sucking gnats commonly known as Sand Flies. The females of these small (one-and-a-half to four-mm-long) flies have piercing-sucking mouth parts and are blood suckers that feed on many animals, including humans. They are active only at night when

**Sand Fly**

there is practically no wind. They are very weak, noiseless fliers, and move in short hops of several inches. They seek shelter in dark protected areas and often invade cabins or tents, usually hiding in dark corners, and feed only after the sun has set. They can usually get through normal screens and insect nets.

**Distribution and Habitat:** Sand flies are widely distributed worldwide wherever breeding places combining darkness, humidity, and decaying organic matter are available.

**Symptoms:** Similar to those of "no-see-ums," itchy raised bumps that itch for several hours, some delayed lumps. In some parts of the world, sand flies transmit a number of diseases such as Carrion's disease, leishmaniasis, and sand fly fever. Leishmaniasis has been reported in tropical Mexico and Central America. Northern species don't carry disease.

**Prevention and Control:** Space sprays are very effective against these very weak fliers, and phlebotimine flies are very sensitive to residual sprays as well. Very fine netting sprayed with repellent is also highly effective, as is personal protection with "deet."

**First Aid and Medical Treatment:** Similar to that of other gnats and small flies.

## Horseflies (Tabanidae), Deerflies (Chrysops), and Stable Flies (Muscidae)

Large, biting, blood-sucking flies are among the most annoyingly persistent pests. Their bites are instantly painful, as they imbed their bayonet-like stylets into the skin with a strong thrust of their bodies. Stable Flies make even larger wounds by scratching with their teeth to encourage blood flow. The narrow feeding tube injects saliva into the wound, and then blood and tissue juices are pumped into the fly's digestive system. If undisturbed, they can suck up a full load of blood in three to four minutes. However, since the bite produces a sharp pain, they usually are brushed away and attack again with remarkable persistence. They are noisy, buzzing, rapid, long-range flies. Only the females suck blood, and they bite only during the day. Stable Flies are only as big as their cousins the common housefly (both are of the family Muscidae), but have broader abdomens and are usually found around barns and other places where domestic animals are found. Another predator on warm-blooded animals is the Deerfly. This fly is larger (about ten mm long), more vicious, more numerous, and even more persistent than the Stable Fly and, like the Stable Fly, can transmit disease from animals to humans. The largest of the biting flies, the Horsefly, is about 20 mm long and attacks both domestic animals and humans. It is noisy, large, and slow, and is easily swatted into oblivion. There are over a hundred species of these nasty, biting tabanid flies. They are stout-bodied, with large, often banded, colorful eyes; hence, some are called "green heads." Among them is the famous "blue tail fly" of folk song fame. Deerflies can be distinguished by large yellow spots on a black abdomen.

**Distribution and Habitat:** Wherever domestic and wild, warm-blooded animals are found—often on green fields, beaches, and meadows.

**Symptoms:** Immediate sharp, highly localized pain at site of the bite that may leave a tiny red macule where blood leaked into the bite area. This is followed within several minutes by a raised inflamed red patch that is painful and sometimes itchy for an hour or so. Hours to days later, the bite may form a delayed immune-type skin reaction with local swelling.

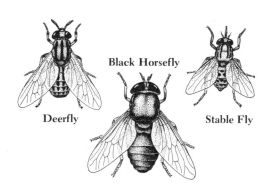

**Black Horsefly**

**Deerfly**

**Stable Fly**

Diseases transmitted by these flies are numerous. For example, there was a recent outbreak of "deerfly fever" or pneumonic tularemia on Martha's Vineyard, Massachusetts. Other diseases transmitted by these flies include anthrax and Loa Loa.

**Prevention and Control:** Space sprays don't do much good because these insects are all strong fliers that cover considerable distances. Repellents are effective, particularly those with high "deet" contents. Their mouth parts are powerful enough to pierce single layers of fabric; hence, layered clothes afford more protection.

**First Aid:** Local symptomatic.

**Medical Treatment:** Local symptomatic.

## *Mosquitoes: Can Transmit Lethal Diseases*

Mosquitoes, dipteran insects of the family Culicidae, are long-legged, slender, delicate, humpbacked pests that are widely distributed from just below the Arctic Circle to the Equator. The females have a long piercing proboscis with which they suck blood and leave itchy, swollen wheals. Most of the time they are simply a persistent annoyance, but some also transmit deadly diseases: malaria, dengue fever, and yellow fever. There are 34 genera and 2700 species of mosquitoes, but we will concentrate on only three genera that are commonly encountered: *Anopheles, Culex,* and *Aedes.*

All these mosquitoes lay rafts of eggs in standing water, and these eggs hatch into air-breathing larvae called wrigglers. After several molts, the wrigglers form pupae that attach themselves to the water surface prior to emerging as adults. The adult female usually mates within a few days after emerging, and then sets out, seeking a blood meal. Her hunting is activated by sensors that respond to the concentration of carbon dioxide in the air. Once airborne, she is attracted to warm, moist objects. Once on the skin, she decides whether to feed. The piercing-sucking organ, the long proboscis, houses a collection of piercing stylets which form a sucking tube. Penetration takes from 30 to 50 seconds, and blood sucking may last for a bit more than two minutes. Withdrawal of the proboscis takes only five seconds, and a female with an abdomen full of blood flies off and won't feed again for two days.

The largest mosquitoes, the black and white gallinippers, are

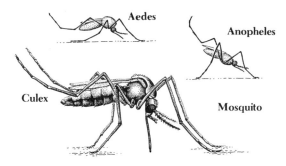

found in the eastern United States from Canada to Mexico. They breed in puddles or water left in marshes at the high spring tides. Like most mosquitoes, they are most active at night and they produce a buzzing song which to most of us is about as pleasant as a fingernail drawn along a blackboard. There are a number of salt-marsh mosquitoes of the genus *Aedes,* some of which fly only short distances, a mile or so, from their breeding grounds, while others can cover 75 miles in six weeks. Some mosquitoes, such as *Culex quinquefasciatus,* the Southern House Mosquito, and the Yellow Fever Mosquito, *Aedes aegypti,* breed indoors in flower vases, water pitchers, or any standing water. Both *Culex* and *Aedes* mosquitoes have their bodies parallel to the surface when they feed, but the *Anopheles* mosquitoes hold their proboscides and bodies in a straight line and look like tiny nails being driven in at an angle into the skin.

**Distribution and Habitat:** Almost everywhere where breeding sites are present. There are practically no yellow fever or malaria transmissions in the United States or Canada.

**Prevention and Control:** Space sprayers or foggers may provide a campsite with temporary relief, but best results are obtained with mechanical barriers such as layered clothing and netting or screens. In heavily infested areas, repellents sprayed on clothing and netting help because some mosquitoes can get their proboscides through thin, tight fabrics. Repellents don't stop biting but do prevent landing. They apparently act by blocking the mosquitoes' sensory apparatus. Good repellents containing "deet" will provide a few hours of protection.

**Symptoms:** Mosquitoes inject their saliva when they have a meal, and this always produces a local swelling that is going to itch, and you will scratch and sometimes cause a secondary infection. Some people who have been bitten frequently may develop a degree of immunity to local mosquitoes but may still react to foreign species. Some individuals have very strong reactions and considerable swelling beyond the bite area.

**First Aid:** Keep bitten areas clean with soap and water, use antiseptics on scratches. Ice packs, anesthetic creams, oral antihistamines, and topical cortisone creams may afford some temporary relief, but in the long run only doctor time will relieve the itch.

## Poisonous Caterpillars (Lepidoptera)

The insect order Lepidoptera, which means scale-winged, includes moths and butterflies. Some of these produce larval forms—caterpillars—which possess poisonous stinging (urticating) hairs. These poisonous hairs are found in the Io Moth caterpillar, Brown-Tail Moth caterpillar, some Flannel Moth caterpillars, and recently have also been reported for the Gypsy Moth caterpillar. The usual cause of trouble is direct contact with the caterpillar or by contact or inhalation of airborne hairs released from a dessicated dead caterpillar. The effects of these hairs is similar to the irritation caused by stinging nettles. The urticating caterpillars are described in the following section.

### *Io Moth Caterpillars* (Automeris Io)

The *Automeris Io* caterpillar is the larva of the Io Moth, which belongs to the moth family Saturniidae. A full-grown caterpillar is about five to eight cm (two to three inches) long, pale green, with lateral strips of red or maroon over white running the length of the body. Near the center of each body segment is a partial row of tubercles armed with radiating green and black spines. Many of these spines are venomous, and their tips are connected to rather large poison glands. (**Plate 31** shows a related Central American species.)

**Distribution:** In the United States, the Io Moth is found in the states east of the Rocky Mountains.

**Habitat and Behavior:** Io moth larvae feed on the leaves of a variety of plants, including corn and willow. In most areas they produce only one annual generation, emerging as a moth in the spring or summer and overwintering as a pupa. In south Texas,

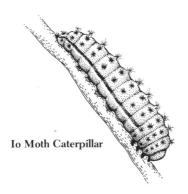

**Io Moth Caterpillar**

however, two generations occur, with one developing in May to July and the second in October to December. Therefore, the larval stages can be found any time from early spring to late fall, depending upon the area of the country and climatic conditions. As with most poisonous caterpillars, *A. io* poisoning occurs when the victim inadvertently contacts caterpillar-infested vegetation. At the instant the victim's skin touches this caterpillar, the spine tips break off in the skin, thus allowing toxin to flow out of the hollow spines and onto the skin.

**Avoidance and Control:** Wear gloves, a long-sleeved shirt, and long pants when working in an infested area. Children should be warned not to handle caterpillars. If necessary, infested vegetation may be treated with an appropriate insecticide.

**Symptoms:** Immediate severe burning pain, followed by local numbness and swelling of the area affected, with severe radiating pain. There is often a double row of parallel red punctuate marks forming a gridlike track along the path of the caterpillar. Sometimes there is swelling of regional lymph nodes downstream (toward the heart) from the stung area. Late foreign-body reaction to unremoved spines can produce pustules. Systemic reactions include: nausea, vomiting, fever, headaches, shock, and convulsions (rare). No deaths have been reported.

**First Aid:** (1) Repeated stripping, using adhesive or cellophane tape to remove spines, (2) The application of ice packs to the inflamed area, and (3) The application of baking soda and water paste.

**Medical Treatment:** For severe pain, give meperidine hydrochloride (Demerol, 50 to 100 mg PO or IM), morphine sulfate (0.25 subcutaneous), codeine phosphate (0.5 g PO). NOTE: Aspirin is generally not effective. If anaphylaxis develops, use standard treatment to counter shock.

## *Puss Caterpillars* (Megalopyge opercularis)

The Puss Caterpillar is the larva of a group commonly referred to as "flannel moths." In some parts of the United States the larva is incorrectly referred to as an "asp." When fully mature, the larvae are near white to dark gray in color, two to three cm (0.8 to 1.2 in.) long, and completely covered with hairs that resemble long tufts of cotton. Some of the hairs are poisonous, and when they penetrate the skin a "toxin" passes from an underlying gland through the hairs at the points of contact. The color variation of the larvae in this species is dependent upon larval age, locality, and time of year. In Texas, where this species is most abundant, the spring/summer generation of caterpillars is usually lighter in color than the fall generation.

**Distribution:** This species has been recorded primarily from the southeastern States, including Alabama, Arkansas, Florida, Georgia, Louisiana, Maryland, Mississippi, Missouri, North Carolina, South Carolina, Texas, and Virginia.

**Habitat and Behavior:** In most of the southern area of its range, the Puss Caterpillar is thought to have two generations per year. The first generation develops in the spring and early summer, while the second generation develops in the fall. After emerging from a cocoon and mating, the female moth lays her eggs on a suitable host plant. In a few days, the eggs hatch into larvae, which develop by feeding on the leaves of a wide range of trees

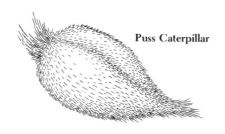

Puss Caterpillar

and shrubs. The natural enemies of the Puss Caterpillar usually keep its numbers under control; however, every four to five years the caterpillars become more numerous, and the number of poisonings associated with them increases.

**Avoidance and Control:** Always wear protective clothing such as gloves and a long-sleeved shirt when working in areas heavily infested with puss caterpillars. During periods of *M. opercularis* abundance, children should be instructed to stay away from infested trees and shrubs and not to handle caterpillars. If necessary, heavy Puss Caterpillar infestations may be treated with an appropriate insecticide.

**Symptoms, First Aid, and Medical Treatment:** The same as for *Automeris io.*

## *Saddleback Caterpillars* (Sibine stimulea)

The saddleback caterpillar is easy to recognize, since its brown, slug-like body is covered mid-dorsally with markings that resemble a brown or purplish saddle sitting on a green and white saddle blanket. Upon close examination, stout spines can be observed along the caterpillar's lateral body margin and on its four tubercles. Many of these spines are hairs that are connected at their bases with individual poison glands. Just prior to pupation and subsequent development into a moth, the caterpillar is two to three cm (0.8 to 1.2 in.) long.

**Distribution:** In general, the Saddleback Caterpillar in the United States is distributed southeast of a diagonal line drawn from Massachusetts through the middle of Texas.

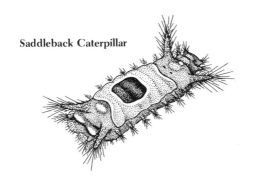

Saddleback Caterpillar

**Habitat and Behavior:** From May to November, *Sibine stimulea* caterpillars may be found feeding on the leaves of a large variety of trees, shrubs, and other plants. Envenomization usually occurs when the victim accidentally contacts vegetation infested with these caterpillars. At the instant the victim's skin contacts the caterpillar, the spine tips break off, thus allowing toxin to flow out of the hollow spines and into or onto the skin.

**Avoidance and Control:** When working in infested areas, wear gloves, a long-sleeved shirt, and long pants to prevent accidental envenomization. During periods of local heavy infestations, children should be instructed to avoid trees, shrubs, and other vegetation commonly infested with these caterpillars. Local entomologists may be contacted to obtain information on the most effective insecticide for Saddleback Caterpillar control in a given area.

**Symptoms, First Aid, and Medical Treatment:** The same as for *Automeris io*.

## Beetles (Coleoptera)

Beetles are sheath-winged insects that occupy a great variety of habitats and comprise the largest order of insects; approximately 40 percent of all insects are beetles. Only two types of beetles directly harm humans, but many indirectly affect us as destructive pests on plants. The North American species that are harmful because they secrete a blister-forming (vesicating) agent belong to the family Meloidae.

### Blister Beetles (Meloidae): Never Lethal

The Meloidae are narrow, elongate beetles characterized by a "neck" (pronotum) which is distinctly narrower than its head or wings. Adult beetles range in body length from one to two cm (0.4 to 0.8 in.) and vary considerably in their coloration.

**Distribution:** In general, Blister Beetles are found in greater numbers in the eastern half of the United States.

**Habitat and Behavior:** The immature stages of the blister beetle usually feed on other insects and are not harmful to man, but adult Blister Beetles release a clear amber fluid by rupture of thin membranes in the leg joints or other segmented areas of the body. This fluid, containing a vesicating (blister-causing) agent called

Blister Beetle

cantharadin, is triggered by pressure against the body of the beetle. Light pressure exerted by clothing or by brushing off a beetle is usually sufficient to cause the release of its vesicating fluid. The adult Blister Beetles are readily attracted to bright white light, and many cases of human exposure occur at night around such lights. Since the adults are plant feeders, some cases of human vesication occur as persons move through vegetation infested with Blister Beetles.

**Avoidance and Control:** In areas with an abundance of Blister Beetles, use yellow light bulbs for outdoor lighting. If a meloid beetle lands on the skin, blow it off; do not crush it. Since cantharidin is distributed throughout the beetle's body, crushing the beetle against exposed skin would result in maximum cantharidin exposure. Skin irritation resulting from Blister Beetle contact is seasonal, with the greatest number of vesicating incidents in the United States occurring in July, August, and September.

**Symptoms:** The reaction generally consists of a superficial line of blisters on the skin. These blisters do not require emergency treatment.

## Lice (Anoplura)

Lice are blood-sucking, wingless, minute, dorso-ventrally-flattened external parasites. They have effective piercing-sucking mouth parts which are retracted into the head when not in use. The ends of their legs are equipped with a curved claw with which these pests cling to hairs of their host. Lice fasten their eggs to hairs with a glue-like substance. These tiny attached eggs are called nits; hence, the expression "nit-picker" had its origin with lice. There are three anoplura that parasitize humans: the Head

Crab Louse

Human Body
Louse

Hog Louse

Louse (*Pediculus humanus capitis*), the Body Louse (*Pediculus humanus corporis*), and the Crab Louse (*Phthirus pubis*).

Several important human diseases have been transmitted from person to person by such lice. These include typhus, relapsing fever, and trench fever. However, most human infestations just produce intense itching.

**Distribution:** Anywhere humans are, and infestation can result from contact with bedding, toilet seats, and by sexual intercourse. Clothing is a good vehicle for transmission to a new host, since eggs are sometimes laid in fabric.

**Symptoms:** Infestation with lice, sometimes called pediculosis, produces intense itching, and in very severe cases of chronic infestation, skin damage and anemia. Sometimes the scalp becomes encrusted due to secondary infection.

**Prevention and Control:** Spray suspected areas with sprays containing malathion (2 percent). Lice can be detected by using ultraviolet light, since lice fluoresce white under this light and their movement can be seen.

**Treatment:** A 1 percent gamma benzene hexachloride cream applied for several days will get rid of the infestation. Retreatment one week later may be needed.

## Fleas (Siphonaptera)

Fleas are minute, hard-bodied, eyeless, wingless insects that are flattened bilaterally. They have piercing-sucking mouthparts with which they suck blood. Females require blood to form their eggs.

The eggs eventually fall off the host and fall into resting places (sand, flooring, rugs, etc.). The whitish active larvae feed on organic debris and then form cocoons from which they eventually emerge as adult fleas. The adults can remain quiescent in the cocoons for weeks. Fleas are very susceptible to dryness and thrive best in a high humidity. They are quite resistant to cold (about −1°C); hence, they can over winter in a state of suspended animation.

Fleas have been around in their present form for at least 50 million years, and some 1500 species of fleas are known. They have evolved powerful jumping legs to aid them in reaching their host. The jump of the flea is lightning fast, too fast for the human eye to follow. Fleas weigh less than a thousandth of a gram, are about one or two millimeters long, and can jump a hundred times their own body length. Human Fleas can execute standing jumps of more than one foot. They seem to be tireless and have been reported to jump 600 times per hour for as long as 72 hours. In the jump the flea may somersault or spin while airborne, but most of the time they land on their feet. Cat Fleas (*Ctenocephalus felis*), Dog Fleas (*C. canis*), Human Fleas (*Pulex irritans*), and Rat Fleas (*Xenopsylla cheopis*) all attack humans, the last mentioned being the transmitter of the dreaded bubonic plague that killed millions of people during the middle ages.

**Distribution:** Fleas can be encountered across all of North America but thrive best in humid areas.

**Habitat and Behavior:** Although eggs are laid on their hosts, they fall off and hatch in places where the host spends the most time. Indoors these may include chairs, rugs, floor crevices, and outdoors in the soil or sand. The larval fleas hatch into maturity and can live for many weeks without food. Fleas have impressive host-finding capabilities, responding to temperature, carbon dioxide from the exhaled breath, or odor. The Human Flea also is

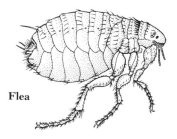

**Flea**

particularly attracted to females, and seems to respond to female hormones. Once on the host, they use their piercing-sucking mouth parts to suck blood. The flea's saliva being a foreign protein causes painful itchy inflammation at the site of the bite.

**Symptoms:** Flea bites are both painful and itchy, and the irritation may last for several days to a week or longer.

**Treatment:** Use topical cortisone cream (non-prescription) to limit the inflammation, and commercially available anti-itch creams which contain local anesthetics such as benzocaine to control the itch. Follow instructions on medication. The main thing to do is prevent further bites by controlling the fleas.

**Control:** Apply surface sprays containing methoxychlor, malathion, pyrethrins, or ronnel. Be careful to use a nonstaining spray when spraying furniture or carpets. Treat baseboards, cracks in the floor, furniture, and other places where pets usually sleep. Since pets are the usual source of fleas, it is important to control infestations on pets by the usual commercially available dusts containing 5 percent malathion or methoxychlor. Flea collars are also helpful.

## Bedbugs (Cimicidae)

The most important of the bloodsucking true bugs are the bedbugs, which probably first became acquainted with man when he shared caves with bats and swallows during the Ice Age, and which have since become fully domestic.

The two species that attack humans are *Cimex lectularius*, the common bedbug, and *Cimex hemipterus* (formerly *rotundatus*), or the Indian bedbug. *C. lectularius* is found throughout the temperate regions of the world, while *C. hemipterus* is the abundant tropical bedbug. Bedbugs hibernate and do not feed in cold weather, but remain in a semi-torpid condition. In warm climates they are active all year around. *C. lectularius* is, however, sensitive to temperature above 96° and if the humidity is high, they die.

Bedbugs are round, flat insects of a rich reddish-brown

Bedbug

mahogany color, which has led to their being called "Mahogany Flats." They have short, broad heads with prominent compound eyes, long four-segmented antennae and a three-segmented beak or proboscis. Their legs are well developed and they can crawl up vertical surfaces with little difficulty. Bedbugs are almost wingless and are four to five millimeters long when fully grown. One of the most striking characteristics of bedbugs is their peculiar foul pungent odor produced by "stink glands" located at the base of the hind legs. Bedbugs have piercing and sucking mouthparts which are folded back under the head and thorax when not in use and extend downward at a right angle to the body when the bug is feeding. As the bedbug feeds, it injects saliva which has the effect of partly digesting the food and so making it more fluid. The saliva also contains an anticoagulant. Bedbugs seldom cling to the skin while sucking, preferring to remain on the clothing.

Bedbugs are night prowlers, hiding away in cracks and crevices during the daytime. Favorite hiding places are in bedsteads, in the crevices between boards, under wallpaper and similar places for which their flat bodies are eminently adapted. They sometimes go considerable distances to hide in the daytime, and show remarkable resourcefulness in reaching sleepers at night. In fact, most of their activity is directed toward searching for a host. The antennae are held out straight in front of the head and evidence suggests that they are guided toward a suitable host by following up a temperature gradient.

**Symptoms:** Although some people seem to be immune to the effects of bedbug bites, others experience considerable irritation. Children suffer most from bedbug bites. In susceptible persons there is severe irritation caused by the salivary secretion. The bite produces a swollen, itchy, red blotch, with a central spot. In severe cases there may be a marked nervous reaction accompanied by digestive disorders and loss of sleep.

**First Aid:** Because bedbugs attack at night while the host is asleep, it is not really possible to administer immediate first aid. There is nothing that can be done but treat the symptoms by applying calamine lotion, mild analgesics, or a paste of baking soda and cold cream or a compress moistened with a diluted solution of ammonia.

**Prevention and Control:** Prevention of bedbug infestation consists chiefly in good housekeeping, but occasional temporary infestations are likely to occur in almost any inhabited building. Rooms should be cleaned and kept free from cracks; metal bedsteads offer considerable obstacles to the bedbug. To destroy this pest, wet the cracks of the bedstead and other places in which it hides with 5 percent lindane, malathion, or pyrethrum. In bad infestations, fumigation with hydrocyanic acid gas is the surest method but is only safe when used by experienced operators. Several repetitions at weekly intervals will kill newly hatched bugs.

## Assassin Bugs (Reduviidae)

There are more than four thousand species of Reduviidae, a family that usually feeds on insects but in some cases feeds on humans. One close relative of the insect assassins, the Triatomas, not only feed on human blood but spread a parasitic disease (Chagas disease) in South America. Like all true bugs, the reduviids live on a fluid diet (plant juices or animal blood). To obtain this food, these sucking insects use a beak or proboscis that pushes a set of sharp, hollow, hypodermic-like piercing stylets through the skin. The bug then squirts in a venomous saliva that contains enzymes that break down fats and tissues, thus liquifying them so that they can be sucked in. In animals, the main effects of the poison is to release histamine, a potent vasodilator. The venom is also a potent antigen, and because of this the bite can produce extremely severe allergic reactions to victims exposed previously to bites by these insects. There are two reduviids common to North America that attack humans. These are the Conenose Bugs and the Wheel Bugs.

## Conenose or Kissing Bugs (*Triatoma*)

Species of the genus *Triatoma* have the elongate (cone-shaped) head which is characteristic of the family Reduviidae. Hence, the name "conenose bugs" is often used to describe these insects. They range in color from light brown to black and may exhibit checkerboard-like orange and black markings where the abdomen extends laterally past the folded wings. These insects are flattened dorsally, which allows them to hide in small cracks and crevices.

**Assassin Bug**

The size of mature adults varies from approximately one to three cm (0.4 to 1.2 in.) in length, depending upon the species.

**Distribution:** *Triatoma* species that attack humans are generally located in the southern half of the United States. *Triatoma* feeds exclusively on vertebrate blood; hence, it nests close to its source of food, such as bird nests, animal lairs, barns, and houses inhabited by humans and pets.

**Biology/Behavior:** Conenose bugs are nocturnal insects. They take their blood meals at night and hide in any available crack or crevice between feedings. Assassin bugs, as a group, normally feed on small mammals, but in the absence of their preferred hosts, several species will readily feed on humans. The proboscis contains four piercing stylets that easily penetrate the skin without producing any initial pain. They are commonly referred to as "kissing bugs" because in 1899 a woman in Washington, D.C., was bitten on the lip by a *triatoma*, which led to wide newspaper coverage and a nationwide hysteria about "kissing bugs." Some of the common sites of human attack, in order of frequency, are the hands, arms, feet, head, and trunk. If hosts are available, these bugs feed every three or four days, but these Conenoses can survive for several months without feeding. In warmer climates, they remain active throughout the year. While the bite itself is painless, the reduviid, when startled while feeding, will quickly withdraw its mouthparts, causing a severe, painful wound.

**Symptoms:** *Triatoma* bites produce a spectrum of allergic reactions which are dependent on previous history of bites by these pests and subsequent sensitization. The lesions—and there may be a cluster of them—are more severe than more common insect bites and consist of swollen, red, pimple-like eruptions with a central dot of blood. In sensitized individuals, giant urticarial lesions with a central puncture occur as a generalized reaction. Sometimes a delayed reaction several days after the bite produces hemorrhagic nodular to bulbous lesions of the hand or foot.

**First Aid:** Local wound care, topical corticosteroids, and antihistamines will relieve inflammation. Analgesics may help relieve the pain.

**Medical Treatment:** If secondary infection develops, treat with antibiotic. If an abscess forms due to remnants of stylets left in the wound, drain, elevate extremity, and use local heat to increase circulation in the area of the lesion. If anaphylaxis develops, treat the same as hymenoptera stings (see p. 113).

## Wheel Bugs (*Arilus cristatus*)

The Wheel Bug, *Arilus cristatus*, has the typical small, narrow head characteristic of the Reduviidae family. They are mouse gray in color and are approximately 2.5 to 4 cm (1 to 1.6 in.) long. A cogwheel-like crest on the dorsal side of the prothorax is distinctive to this insect and accounts for its popular name, "wheel bug."

**Distribution:** Wheel Bugs are generally found in the southern two-thirds of the United States.

**Biology/Behavior:** Wheel Bugs are usually predators on soft-bodied insects, and human bites are usually the result of accidental contact while handling vegetation, boards, or other objects. The bug penetrates the skin with its "beak," or proboscis, and injects a potent venomous secretion normally used in killing its insect prey.

**Avoidance and Control:** The best way to prevent Wheel Bug contact is to be able to identify this unusual insect and avoid it. Children should be instructed not to handle it. Wearing leather gloves while working outside will prevent bites which occur when the Wheel Bug is accidently picked up with vegetation or other debris. Since Wheel Bugs are predacious on many harmful insects and are generally considered beneficial, control is not recommended.

**Symptoms:** Wheel Bug bites are characterized by immediate intense pain which usually subsides in from three to six hours.

**First Aid:** Local wound care, topical corticosteroids, and antihistamines will relieve inflammation. Analgesics may help relieve the pain.

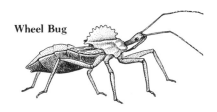

Wheel Bug

**Medical Treatment:** If secondary infection develops, treat with antibiotic. If an abscess forms due to remnants of stylets left in the wound, drain, elevate extremity, and use local heat to increase circulation in the area of the lesion. If anaphylaxis develops, treat the same as Hymenoptera stings (see p. 113).

## Giant Water Bugs (Belostomidae)

One of the hemipterans that has adapted to a freshwater environment is the Giant Water Bug (Belostomidae). These bugs have not developed gills and frequently come to the surface for air. These immense predators are also strong flyers and can fly from one water body to another. They are attracted to light and are sometimes called "electric light bugs." They are so powerful that they have been known to kill frogs and will even attack birds encountered in flight. Their offensive weapon is a very strong retractable beak which can inflict a very painful wound. These insects can reach lengths of up to ten cm, are brownish and may be encountered in the water (they are powerful swimmers) or around lighted camp sites.

**Distribution:** Most bodies of fresh water from southern Canada to Panama.

**Habitat and Behavior:** Freshwater ponds or campsites that are well lighted. Human bites are relatively rare.

**Symptoms:** An immediate sharp pain, minor inflammation.

**First Aid:** Treat as you would any insect sting.

**Medical Treatment:** None.

**Giant Water Bug**

# PART VI
# *Other Venomous Invertebrate Animals*

## Leeches (Hirudinea)

Leeches are predators that can also be referred to as external parasites because they attach themselves to their prey by means of suckers. Their bodies generally have 34 segments which give their exteriors a segmented or ringed appearance. Unlike other annelid worms, leeches lack bristles or setae. They have a powerful, elaborate musculature which allows them to stretch out and shorten dramatically. This musculature allows leeches to both creep along the bottom and to swim with graceful undulations.

Within the anterior sucker is a jawed mouth. Once the mouth is attached, the teeth make a painless trifid incision into which is secreted a potent anticoagulant called hirudin. One resident blood-sucking species, *Macrobdella,* is found to infest swimming holes, ponds, and lakes and preys on both humans and pets.

**Distribution:** Fresh-water bodies from Maine to Minnesota, from Pennsylvania to Kansas northward into Canada.

**Habitat and Behavior:** Leeches abound in fresh-water ponds and lakes, and some are even found in fresh-water streams. Most are nocturnal, hiding under stones or in the mud during the day. When stimulated by hunger or the proximity of food, probably detected by smell, they attach themselves to the skin and quickly extract more than their own weight of the host's blood. This rapid

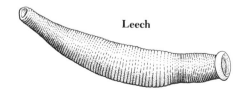

**Leech**

blood-sucking is aided by a powerful muscular pharynx. During such feeding the Leech balloons. Leeches may be readily pulled off manually, although people who are reluctant to touch them can cause them to voluntarily let go by copiously sprinkling them with table salt. Leeches have been used medicinally to decrease swelling such as happens after a black eye. They were kept by barbershops of the early part of this century for that purpose.

**Symptoms:** A small incision in the skin that bleeds profusely for a while after the leech is removed. There is usually little or no pain. Small children who spend lots of time sitting in pond shallows may suffer multiple attacks, which could produce serious blood loss.

**First Aid:** Apply a gauze bandage with firm pressure until clot forms and keep wound area clean. No medical treatment is called for unless the lesion becomes infected.

## Marine Annelid Worms That Bite or Envenomate

Annelids are the most highly developed segmented worm-like invertebrate animals. The largest and oldest class of the annelids are the marine polychaet worms, of which there are some ten thousand species, most of them marine forms. Some are small, 1/25 of an inch long; some are large, almost ten feet long; and at least two can cause some human pain by either biting or stinging and injecting venom. (**Plate 20.**)

Glycera dibranchiata, "the beak thrower" or "bloodworm," has a pointed head adapted for burrowing but can evert its head and bite down with two pairs of beak-like jaws. The bite usually leaves four puncture marks, forming an oval wound, and there may be a

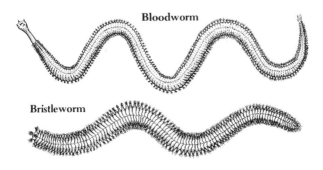

Bloodworm

Bristleworm

toxic component which produces some pain, redness, and swelling. Fisherman handling these potential bait worms can avoid being bitten by wearing gloves.

All polychaet annelids have hardened hair-like projections or bristles called setae on each segment. The setae function in swimming, in gripping surfaces, and in defense or offense. Two families of polychaets, the Amphinomidae and the Chryopetalidae, are referred to as "fire worms" or "bristle worms" because their hollow, glass-like, venom-filled setae can penetrate the skin and cause a painful, itchy skin irritation. The tiny venom-filled setae often break off in the skin, so the inflammation may persist for some hours.

**Distribution and Habitat:** "Fire Worms," such as *Eurythöe complanata* and *Hermodice carunculata*, are predators found in shallow marine waters under rocks or driftwood or among kelp holdfasts in the Gulf of Mexico. Biting worms such as the "beak thrower" are burrowing bottom dwellers found in muddy or sandy flats from the Atlantic Coast of Canada to North Carolina. Victims of their bites are usually fishermen using them as bait.

**Prevention:** A simple mechanical barrier such as work gloves is sufficient to prevent either bites or spine penetration.

**First Aid:** Clean wound and treat as you would urticating caterpillar wounds, using adhesive tape to pull out imbedded setae (see P. 135). Topical corticosteroid creams can lessen the symptoms. If a secondary infection occurs, consult a physician.

## Stinging Cnidaria

Coelenterates are primitive two-layered animals equipped with a hollow cul-de-sac bowel from which they derive their name. One division of the Coelenterates are the Cnidaria, all of which have a specialized stinging apparatus. There are three relevant orders of cnidarians. These are the Hydrozoa, which includes the infamous Portuguese Man-of-War; the cup-like order, Scyphozoa, which include the true jellyfish, the annoying sea nettles, and the sometimes deadly Sea Wasps and giant Lion's Mane Jellyfish; and the order Anthozoa, which includes the stinging corals and anemones.

The stinging cells, called nematocysts, are capsular and located within the outer layer of tissue on the tentacles. This poison-filled capsule is structured in such a way that a small portion of its membrane is folded back into its interior, where it evolves into a long, coiled, hollow thread tube with sharp barbs or hooks at its base. The entire nematocyst is then nestled within a second fluid-filled capsule called a cnidoblast. The cnidoblast has a cover or operculum, which acts as a door that is spring-loaded shut. Pressure-sensitive spiny projections from the cnidoblast, called cnidocils, react to contact and open the operculum; the coiled thread tube of nematocyst is then discharged. Its sharp end punctures the skin, while its hooks grip the epidermis. Thus, a conduit is formed between the venom sac of the nematocyst and the skin of the swimmer.

A single brush with a tentacle may produce thousands of these conduits. The nematocysts are arranged in such a way that there are batteries of nematocysts on the tentacle, arranged like "rungs on a ladder." Each battery contains 500 large nematocysts and 2000 smaller ones. The main tentacle of the Man-of-War may contain 750,000 nematocysts! The tentacles sway back and forth in the water, and if something touches them they are activated and release a venom. The amount of toxin released is proportional to the number of nematocysts activated. The larger the number of tentacles, and the greater surface area per tentacle touched, the more nematocysts will be activated.

In theory, any Coelenterate equipped with nematocysts is capable of stinging. However, the effect of the sting is dependent upon a multitude of factors. Most importantly, different Coelenterates have different stinging capabilities. Their effects range from mild dermatitis to almost instant death. Furthermore, within a given order of Coelenterata different members have varying types of nematocysts, each having a different degree of penetrating power. Those with little ability to penetrate the skin or those which rarely dislodge the entire stinging apparatus in the victim will have a relatively mild effect, independent of the potency of the toxin. The amount of exposed area and the length of time which the tentacles are in contact with the skin will also determine the effects of the skin. Finally, some people, because of their physiology or previous exposure, are known to be more sensitive to the Coelenterate venoms.

## The Portuguese Man-of-War (*Physalia physalis*)

Probably the most commonly encountered stinging jellyfish is the conspicuous Portuguese Man-of-War, found floating by the tens of thousands off the southern Atlantic and Gulf coasts. Actually *Physalia physalis* is not a jellyfish but a colony of hydroid polyps hanging from a gas-filled float. The float or pneumatophore is a

Portuguese
Man-of-war

translucent bladder tinted with blue, pink, and purple and filled
with nitrogen (75 percent), oxygen (14 percent), carbon monoxide
(9 percent) and other gases. It is from five to 15 inches long and
may project out of the water by seven or eight inches. The float
acts like a sail; thus *Physalia,* unlike the true jellyfish, can't swim,
but is completely at the mercy of the currents and winds. Hanging
below the float is a tangle of tentacles that may trail 30 feet or
more behind. The tentacles have reproductive individuals, digesting individuals, and stinging individuals. (**Plate 22.**)
     Stinging cells, nematocysts, are grouped in batteries around
each tentacle. There are both large and small nematocysts found
along the entire length of the tentacles, and each tentacle may
contain three quarters of a million nematocysts. Nematocysts are
discharged by mechanical and chemical stimuli when the swaying
tentacles or even broken-off floating pieces of tentacle make
contact. The larger the number of tentacles contacted, the greater
the sting.

**Distribution and Habitat:** Warm tropical waters, particularly
common off both the Florida coasts and throughout the West
Indies and Gulf of Mexico. Sometimes after storms thousands are
blown inshore and washed onto beaches as far north as New
England. They generally follow the Gulf Steam.

**Symptoms:** Mildly painful prickling sensations to intense shock-
like burning, throbbing pain. Pain can radiate and even cause
joint muscle throbbing pain. The stung area, usually a long welt
where the tentacle hit, becomes very red and swollen as if the
victim had been thrashed with a whip. The rash may develop tiny
hemorrhages and in some cases becomes numb. In extreme cases,
the victim will develop severe asthma within minutes or may go
into shock. Other symptoms of severe stings include weakness,

chills, fever, nausea, vomiting, cramps, even unconsciousness. Some deaths after a severe encounter are due to loss of consciousness and drowning. Less severe stings can still cause hayfever-like symptoms—coughing, sneezing, runny eyes, sweating, stuffed nose, wheezing, muscle cramps, and tightness of the chest. Previously stung people may become supersensitive to Physalia toxin and go into anaphylactic shock even after minor stings.

**Prevention and Control:** Avoid *Physalia*-infested waters, and if you see many fresh blue bottles up on the beach it's a good idea to put off swimming. Wearing a shirt and pants while swimming provides some protection and, indeed, in Australia where there are some deadly Sea Wasps, swimmers wear panty hose. Wet suits are thick enough to prevent nematocyst penetration.

**First Aid:** According to Dr. Findlay Russell and Dr. Bruce Halstead, anything that will inactivate the nematocysts (which continue to inject poison) is helpful. These include ammonia and vinegar washes of the stung area. Sodium bicarbonate, boric acid, lemon juice, and alcohol have been used effectively for minor stings. If tentacles are stuck to the skin, remove them (wear gloves, or you'll get stung), wash with sea water, pour vinegar, ammonia, alcohol, or formaldehyde over the sting. Then dust with flour or baking powder or even dry sand (do not rub with sand or use fresh water—it causes more poison to be injected), and then scrape off the powder and its adhering nematocysts with a knife. (Do not use a razor, since it cuts off the tips of the imbedded nematocysts.) Wash again with salt water. Topical antiinflammatory cortisone (0.5 percent) is now a nonprescription drug and should relieve local inflammation. Topical pain-killing analgesic balms containing benzocaine also provide some relief. If victim is showing distress of allergic symptoms, get him to a physician.

**Medical Treatment:** Be prepared to treat for shock or respiratory distress. I.V. epinephrine, meperidine for pain, 10 percent Ca gluconate for muscle spasm.

## Sea Blubber (*Cyanea capillata*)

*Cyanea capillata*, commonly called sea blubber by fishermen, is a giant among the jellyfish. It belongs to a class of coelomates called Scyphozoans or cup animals. Cyanea has an enormous bell that averages three feet across, but the largest recorded measured

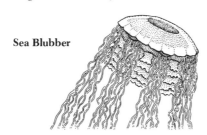

Sea Blubber

twelve feet in diameter. The bell is notched and divided into many lobes. It is yellow-brown, orange, or blue and is thinner at its margins, which contain sense organs. Muscular contractions of the bell provide swimming power. Hanging from the bell are several hundred long tentacles armed with enormous batteries of powerful stinging cells. In large specimens, these reddish or white tentacles trail as much as a hundred feet behind the bell, possibly giving rise to some of the ancient "sea serpent" myths.

Cyanea inhabits cool and cold waters of the open sea off both coasts of North America and are occasionally washed into shallow waters by storm. Contact with the batteries of stinging cells in the tentacles can raise huge painful wheals on the skin.

**Distribution and Habitat:** Cool to cold waters of the open Atlantic from southern Canada to North Carolina, and in the Pacific from the Aleutian Islands to the California coast. Most frequently encountered on the open ocean, they can be blown into more shallow waters.

**Symptoms:** Initial symptoms, similar to those of *Physalia*, which may disappear in a few hours, or in severe cases can cause blistering and loss of tissue. Sometimes after healing, these whip-like wounds leave raised scars or lines of dark pigment that may last for years.

**First Aid, Prevention and Medical Treatment:** The same as for *Physalia*.

## Sea Wasps

The most deadly jellyfish, Sea Wasps, *Chironex fleckeri* and *Chiropsalmus quadrigatus*, fortunately are not found in American waters. In the Indopacific they are responsible for a number of deaths each year, probably more than all shark attacks world-wide. The nematocysts of these true jellyfish contain, among other things, a potent cardiovascular toxin, which in severe stings can produce complete collapse and death within minutes  There are

Sea Wasp

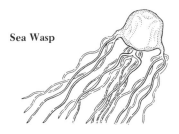

American Sea Wasps, but most, like *Chiropsalmus quadramanus*, found along the coasts of the Gulf of Mexico, are quite small and rarely lethal.

**Habitat and Distribution:** Less dangerous Sea Wasps of American waters are found in the Atlantic from North Carolina southward through the West Indies, and one species is found in the shallow waters of the Gulf.

**Symptoms:** Vary with severity of the sting and are similar to those caused by *Physalia*. Enzymes in jellyfish poison destroy subcutaneous fat cells and cause blister formation and later sloughing of the skin. Where a victim made contact with a tentacle, there can be rapid development of a raised purple welt which later blisters. Healing may be slow, and the wounded area may be intermittently itchy for years. There are frequent reports of scar formation and prolonged darkening of the wounded area.

**First Aid, Prevention, and Medical Treatment:** The same as for *Physalia*.

## Sea Nettles (*Dactylometra quinquecirrha*)

Sea Nettles, *Dactylometra quinquecirrha*, are small (eight-inch-long) jellyfish equipped with three-foot tentacles. Stinging cell batteries are found in both the tentacles and the bell, which is usually either white or pink. These pests, while not really dangerous, can make life miserable for swimmers because they are often found in huge numbers in the less salty waters of bays and estuaries. They are particularly bothersome in Chesapeake Bay and some Carolina sounds. Like all jellyfish, they swim by muscular movements of the bell and have four long (usually milk-white) oral arms hanging down around the mouth. (See cover photo.)

**Sea Nettle**

**Habitat and Distribution:** From the Massachusetts to Florida Atlantic coasts, particularly numerous in warm, less salty waters of estuaries, sounds, and bays.

**Symptoms:** Usually only mildly painful burning, stinging sensation.

**First Aid:** The same as for mild *Physalia* stings.

**Medical Treatment:** None usually required unless the victim shows severe allergic symptoms.

## Stinging Corals (Milleporina)

The stinging corals are false corals of the order Milleporina. They look like true corals and have a massive, yellow-tipped brownish, limestone-like exoskeleton, the upper portions of which contain small craters in which the stinging polyps live. The most common stinging coral is *Millepora alcicornis*, which is found in the warm, tropical waters of the Caribbean Sea, usually living with true corals along the reefs of those waters. (**Plate 27.**)

Upon brushing or pressing against a stinging coral, the victim will experience instantaneous pain which increases in intensity. The pain usually remains sharp for only a few minutes, but it produces small, red welts on the skin, and allergic reactions may occur. In some cases these welts may form small ulcers.

The stinging coral is not particularly dangerous, and its venom is not normally lethal to humans; however, it does represent a danger to divers around the coral.

## Coral Cuts

Rocky corals can cause severe abrasions and cuts. The cuts sometimes contain small bits of coral which act as foreign bodies and can cause festering painful sores that can become infected.

Wet suits and gloves usually are sufficient protection. If coral cuts occur, clean the wound according to accepted first aid practices. If an infection develops consult a physician.

## Fire Sponges

Sponges are primitive animals organized into a variety of cells forming the first evolutionary appearance of tissues. There are over five thousand species of sponges belonging to phylum Porifera. The name Porifera implies that the body has many pores through which water circulates into the sponge's internal chambers. Sponges have unique supportive skeletal systems made up of spiny spicules composed of calcium, silicon, or organic matter. Almost all sponges are found in salty waters and one group of tropical and subtropical sponges gives off a toxic agent which can be dangerous to humans. These are the colorful red and orange fire sponges. (**Plate 28.**)

Fire Sponges envenomate by causing superficial abrasions, probably with their fine-pointed spicules, and the toxin they secrete is then absorbed through the cut. However, Dr. Russell points out that there are recorded cases of the toxin, a complex mix of potentially poisonous substances, absorbed through undamaged skin.

**Habitat and Distribution:** Fire Sponges are found in subtropical and tropical marine waters encrusted as thin bright colorful layers on corals, rocks, and shipwrecks.

**Symptoms:** Within 30 minutes after contact the victim will feel an intense burning and itching sensation usually localized at the point of contact. The skin appears red and swollen and in severe cases sweating, weakness, nausea, loss of sensation, and even fainting are experienced.

**Prevention and Control:** Learn to recognize and avoid Fire Sponges if you are doing any scuba diving or snorkeling. Gloves and wet suits should prevent any effects.

**First Aid and Medical Treatment:** Wash off skin with soapy water and treat symptoms as they occur. Topical over-the-counter cortisol creams may alleviate the burning and itching. Oral antihistamines may also be of benefit and aspirin may reduce some of the pain. If systemic symptoms occur treat them symptomatically.

## Sea Urchins (Echidnoidea): Envenomate, Produce Puncture Wounds; Sometimes Dangerous to Eat

The phylum Echinodermata, spiny skinned animals, includes Starfish, Sea Cucumbers, and Sea Urchins. They are all radially symmetrical animals with a water vascular system to aid in locomotion. While there can be toxic reactions to some Starfish and Sea Cucumbers found in American waters, these are relatively rare and of minor importance, hence will not be discussed here. The Sea Urchins, class Echinoidea, do pose a problem. These animals have a rigid globular or oval calcareous internal skeleton covered with protuberances called tubercules. Attached to these protuberances are brittle, sharp-pointed spines. Some American species such as the West Indian White Sea Urchin, *Tripneustes ventricosus* are equipped with slender, hollow, hypodermic needle-like spines which contain a violet-colored viscous toxin. If these spines penetrate the skin, they usually break off, leaving the venom-filled tip imbedded in the skin, causing considerable localized redness and pain and sometimes a nasty, festering puncture wound. Sometimes the spines are absorbed in a day or two, and sometimes they must be removed surgically. Even spines of non-venomous species of urchins produce puncture wounds with broken pieces of spine that may cause infection if not removed.

Sea Urchins also have modified, small-stalked protective organs, called pedicellaria, all over the body surface between the spines. These structures protect the Sea Urchin from parasites and other small marine organisms that land on its surface. There are several types of pedicellaria (see Dr. F.E. Russell's book, *Poisonous Marine Animals*, for more details) which are equipped with tiny jaws or fang-like structures that when stimulated clamp down and introduce venom produced by glands on the pedicellaria. Often after the jaws close and the pedicellaria are pulled off, the Sea Urchin poison continues to be injected into the victim, causing instant severe pain, redness, and swelling. The entire part envenomated may ache, and in severe cases generalized systemic responses such as nausea and fainting occur. Russell reports that in some cases the victim rapidly experiences loss of sensation and numbness of the mouth, loss of muscle tone (weakness) in the lips, tongue, voice box, eyelids, and even muscles of the arms and legs. These symptoms may last several hours and then subside.

Finally, some species of Sea Urchins during their mating season may produce toxic substances which concentrate in the ovaries, making them dangerous to eat. For those who consider Sea

Urchin roe a gastronomic delicacy the price may be high, since the toxin produces some gastric upset and allergic-like symptoms.

**Distribution and Habitat:** Sea Urchins are found in most shallow waters among rocks, coral, and even on sandy bottoms. Some species have very short spines, while others, particularly those found in warmer tropical and subtropical waters, have spines several inches long. (**Plate 19.**)

**Prevention and Control:** Watch where you put your hands and feet and wear sneakers, although that is no guarantee of protection, since I have had spines go right through the sides of canvas sneakers into my foot. Short-spined tropical species should not be handled without gloves because of the potential for pedicillaria stings.

**First Aid:** Treat spine wounds as any puncture wound and treat pedicellaria stings as you would *Physalia* (p. 153).

**Medical Treatment:** If imbedded spines don't absorb within a day or two, consult a physician. They may have to be removed surgically. If secondary infection occurs, consult a physician. For systemic reactions to pedicellaria envenomation, treat symptomatically.

# SELECTED REFERENCES

ARNOLD, R.E., MD. 1979. "Controversies and Hazards in the Treatment of Pit Viper Bites." Southern Medical Journal, 72 (8):902–10.

BARNARD, J.H. 1973. "Studies of 400 Hymenoptera sting deaths in the United States." Journal of Allergy and Clinical Immunology, 52:259–64.

DITMARS, R.L. 1964. Reptiles of the World. Macmillan, New York.

FRAZIER, C.A. 1968. "Diagnosis and treatment of insect bites." CIBA, 20 (3):75–86. CIBA Pharmaceutical Co., N.J.

HABELMEHL, G.G. 1981. Venomous Animals and Their Toxins. Springer-Verlag, Berlin/New York.

HALSTEAD, BRUCE W. Dangerous Marine Animals. Cambridge, Md.: Cornell Maritime Press, 1959.

———, AND D.A. COURVILLE. Poisonous and Venomous Marine Animals of the World (3 vols.). Washington, DC: Government Printing Office, 1965–70.

KLAUBER, L.M. 1956. Rattle Snakes, Their Habits, Life Histories and Influence on Mankind. University of California Press, Los Angeles.

MINTON, SHERMAN A., JR. Snake Venoms and Envenomation. New York: Marcel Dekker, 1971.

MOORE, G.M. 1965. Poisonous Snakes of the World, a Manual for Use by U.S. Amphibious Forces. U.S. Government Printing Office, Washington, D.C.

PARRISH, H., AND C. CARR. 1967. "Bites by copperheads in the United States." Journal of the American Medical Association, 201:107–12.

———. "Analysis of 460 Fatalities from Venomous Animals in the United States," American Journal of Medical Sciences, 245, No. 2, Feb. 1963.

———. "Deaths from Bites and Stings of Venomous Animals and Insects in the United States," A.M.A. Archives of International Medicine, Vol. 104, Aug. 1959.

———. "Incidence of Treated Snakebites in the United States," Public Health Reports, 81, No. 3, Mar. 1966.

RUSSELL, F.E. 1966. "Injuries by venomous animals." American Journal of Nursing, 66:1322–1326.

———, AND P. SAUNDERS, EDS. 1970. Animal Toxins. The First International Symposium on Animal Toxins. Pergamon Press, London.

———. 1980. Snake Venom Poisoning. Lippincott, Philadelphia.

———, AND PAUL R. SAUNDERS (EDS.). Animal Toxins. New York: Pergamon Press, 1967.

———, AND HAROLD W. PUFFER. "Pharmacology of Snake Venoms," in Snake Venoms and Envenomation, ed. Sherman A. Minton, Jr. New York: Marcel Dekker, 1971.

TRIPLETT, R.F., MD. 1976. "The imported fire ant: Health hazard or nuisance?" Southern Medical Journal, 69:258–9.

# Index